The Little Big Book of
ANIMALS

The Little Big Book of
ANIMALS

MᶜRAE BOOKS

The Little Big Book of Animals
was created and produced by McRae Books Srl
Borgo Santa Croce, 8 – Florence (Italy)
info@mcraebooks.com
www.mcraebooks.com
Publishers: Anne McRae and Marco Nardi

Text: Gill Davies
Graphic Design: Marco Nardi
Layouts: Laura Ottina, Stefania Dragomir
Editing: Anne McRae
Picture Research: Nature Picture Library, Anne McRae
Index: Barbara Caria
Color correction: Julia Mellor
Prepress: Filippo Delle Monarche
Repro: R.A.F. Florence

ISBN 88-6098-000-3

Printed and bound in China, by C&C Offset Printing Co.

CONTENTS

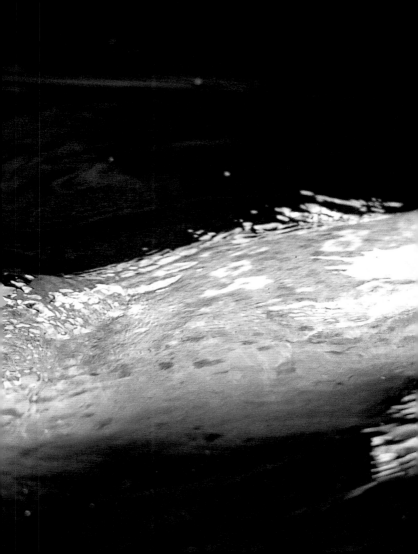

INTRODUCTION

THIS BOOK IS INTENDED AS A VISUAL CELEBRATION OF ANIMALS AND THEIR WAYS OF LIFE. So many of us are fascinated by the creatures that share our planet and it is not hard to understand why: full of vigor and character, they are in many ways easy to identify with and appreciate because they are so much like us. Alternately gentle and fierce, boastful and unassuming, cheeky and shy, or faithful and treacherous, depending on the situation. Think of the ferocity of a lioness defending her offspring, at the same time capable of infinite care and tenderness when moving her tiny cubs in her powerful jaws. Or the eager posturing of a male pheasant or turkey during courtship, and the humility with which some species of male weaver birds prepare nests for some very forthright inspection on the part of prospective female partners.

At the same time, animals are also mysterious and distant, most still inhabitants of a natural world far beyond the confines of urban landscapes and modern lifestyles. Beyond the well-publicized international campaigns to inform us that giant pandas and tigers are endangered or media blitzes covering the plight of stranded whales or miraculous rescues of drowning children by dolphins, most events in the animal world go unrecorded, or at least unreported to the general public. Only a relatively small group of scientists is involved in studying the natural kingdom and there is still much to be discovered.

About two million different animal species have been identified so far but scientists estimate that there are several million more still waiting to be found. As the human population grows, and the spread of farming and forestry intensifies, it seems certain that many species will die out before we make their acquaintance. The latest Red List of Threatened Species, published by the International Union for the Conservation of Nature and Natural Resources (IUCN), estimates that more than 7000 species of animals are at high risk of dying out in the near future. In percentage terms, the numbers are grim: 23 percent of mammal species, 51 percent of reptile species, 40 percent of fishes, and perhaps as many as half of all insect species are believed to be endangered. Triggered by loss of habitat, pollution, and over-exploitation, among other factors, the Earth is currently experiencing a steep decline in biodiversity. Not only is this sad for the loss of so many species of animals, it is also risky for the future of the planet. The loss of many species over a short period of time can influence the overall balance of the natural world and lead to large-scale ecological instability.

In this book we have started out with a fun chapter on animals and their attitudes to life, then gone on to focus on more or less scientific topics, such as their behavior during courtship and mating, the care of offspring, finding food, and strategies for survival. Each chapter begins with a brief introduction and all the photographs are accompanied by succinct captions with snippets of fascinating or fun information. Our aim is to increase awareness of the huge diversity of animal life and behavior and to encourage an interest in preserving this diversity for future generations.

The working title for this chapter was "Animals with Attitude" and the idea was to show how animals can express emotions and states of mind, and how they stand up for themselves, whatever the odds. Anthropomorphic? Maybe, and perhaps some of the captions could be seen as transferring human emotions and ideas to animal expressions. So be it. Animals can't speak

ATTITUDE

in any of our myriad languages, so in many cases we just have to guess at what their gestures or expressions may mean. Many types of behavior, especially among the primates, seem so familiar — parental care and bonding with offspring, for example, — that it is not difficult to assign a meaning. Others are more obscure, and in some cases we have suggested some intriguing options.

p. 29 FITTING IN

This is a male Parson's chameleon from Madagascar. Highly adaptable creatures, chameleons fit in with their surroundings and can "blend into the background."

pp. 30–31 LOVE AND PROTECTION

Baby common marmosets from northeast Brazil, South America. Young siblings find security in each other's company and form close bonds. All the most immediate family members help take care of the young.

TAKING THINGS EASY

A self-assured dominant male gorilla can look pretty laid back and relaxed about life when things are running smoothly but he will quickly become aggressive when attempting to attract a female or trying to show who is boss.
He will beat his chest, jump, kick, and thump nearby vegetation, all the while hooting and roaring.

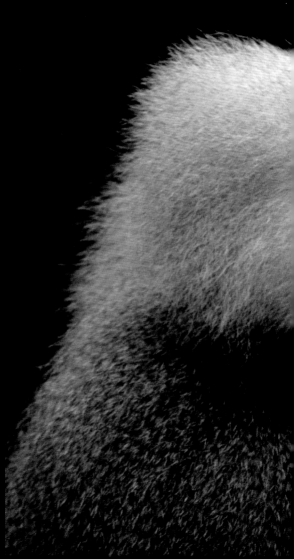

A THREATENING STANCE

A threat display by
a male Hamadryas
baboon from Africa
warns others not to
"push their luck!"
Like all primates,
gorillas have large
brains. This means
they analyze what is
going on around them
and their attitude to
any situation will
depend on many
contributing factors,
not just instinct.
Baboons also have an
excellent memory so
can recall what is
good to eat and
where to find it.

OPPOSITE SEE NO EVIL, HEAR NO EVIL, SPEAK NO EVIL

Japanese macaques live in groups in the forests of Japan.
Famous for washing their food and bathing in hot springs,
they are the subject of many Buddhist myths and are believed to
have inspired the saying "see no evil, hear no evil, speak no evil."

BELOW NOSY MONKEYS

Proboscis monkeys live on the island of Borneo, in Southeast Asia.
They are named for their large, fleshy noses which swell up and
turn red when they are excited.

SEASONAL BEHAVIOR

Attitudes to life vary with the season. In the winter, finding enough food and simply surviving takes precedence for red deer in northern Europe. In the warmer months, however, rutting, mating, and raising young predominate.

Male European mouflon sheep compete for dominance of the herd, posturing, tossing their heads, and fighting numerous battles.

OPPOSITE   A WIN-WIN SITUATION

In the Masai Mara in Kenya, an oxpecker hitches a ride on an impala. Both animals benefit — the bird gets to eat a lot of insects and the impala is spared some irritating itches.

BELOW   GROWING UP

This juvenile mouflon is still growing the strong horns it will need as an adult.

ZEBRAS BARKING

Zebras, like this
Burchell's zebra
from South Africa,
communicate with
each other by making
loud braying sounds,
known as barking. The
sound is described as
somewhere between
the bark of a dog and
the bray of a donkey.

COME ON IN. THE WATER
IS WONDERFUL!

The sea otter of the
North Pacific is well
adapted to enjoying
life in the ocean and
is a brilliant acrobatic
swimmer.

Prairie dogs on the look out. One of the advantages of living in large groups is that there is always a pair of sentries available to check out the area for danger.

BELOW GROUNDHOG DAY

Marmots are a type of rodent. All 14 species live in the Northern hemisphere. The woodchuck, also known as a groundhog, is probably the most famous species of marmot — in the United States it has a holiday named after it. On February 2, Groundhog Day, the animal is believed to emerge from its winter den. If it sees its shadow then it interprets it as an omen of six more weeks of winter weather and returns to its burrow. If it doesn't see its shadow then it stays above ground and spring begins.

With an attitude generally regarded as mean, the grizzly is just one kind of brown bear. All are dangerous and unpredictable — and can be especially aggressive if confronted where there is no opportunity to seek cover.

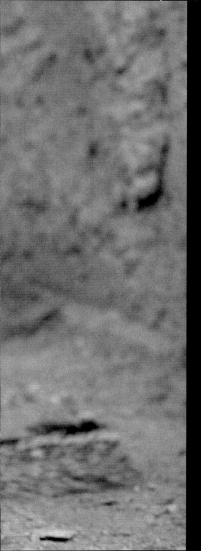

pp. 56–57 CHANGE OF ATTITUDE REQUIRED

In the past, wolves ranged over much of North America, Europe, and Asia. The spread of farming and the belief that wolves will attack and kill both livestock and people led to their being hunted almost to extinction. Recently, attempts have been made to reintroduce them in areas where they were previously exterminated.

TAKING LIFE AS IT COMES

Coyotes simply take what life offers. Making the most of whatever is available, they will eat rodents, rabbits, snakes, insects, carrion, fruit, berries, grasses, fish, frogs, and crabs.

pp. 60–61   TAKING IT EASY

Male lions spend a large part of their time asleep,
leaving the females to do most of the hunting
and to care for offspring.

OPPOSITE AND BELOW   PATIENCE PAYS OFF

European lynx. Waiting and watching . . . the solitary
nocturnal lynx lies in wait in low vegetation or stalks its
prey on the ground. Patience is the name of the game.

pp. 64–65 LEAVE ME ALONE!

Wildcats are secretive creatures whose solitary lifestyle bears little resemblance to either the pampered pet cat or feral cats that live in groups.

CATS OF THE DESERT

Sand cats are about the same size as domestic cats but these hardy little animals are perfectly adapted to life in the harsh conditions of the desert. They don't need to drink because they get all the moisture they need from their food. Their striped yellow fur blends in with their environment and their paws are covered with thick fur to protect them from the burning sands and freezing rocks of the desert. They feed at night on birds, small rodents, snakes and other reptiles, and insects.

PROUD AND REGAL

The tiger, the largest of the big
cats, is a magnificent beast.
The lion may be called the
"king of the jungle" but it is
the tiger that seems to have
the most regal bearing.

LOVING PARENTS

A yawning cheetah mother with her cub in the Masai Mara, Kenya. Like many mammal mothers, cheetahs take care of their offspring for many months after their birth. Not only do they protect them from danger, teach them hunting and other survival skills, but they also engage in behavior that would appear to reflect affection and bonding.

Cheetahs are the fastest animals on land, but only over short distances. However, they seem to accept the fact that their burst of speed is short-lived. If they don't catch the prey straight away, they catch their breaths instead and wait for the next opportunity.

AGGRESSIVE MOMS

Leopards are secretive
creatures that live
alone. They can be
very aggressive when
guarding their
territory and food.
The females are also
aggressively protective
of their young.

Seals and sea lions are the only marine mammals that have not completely severed their links with the land. Brilliant swimmers, they spend most of their time in the water. They come on land to breed and bask in the sun although they look ungainly as they pull themselves along with their flippers.

DON'T BE FOOLED

This beguiling expression might suggest a relaxed attitude to life but in fact, the hippopotamus (this one in the Masai Mara, Kenya) is a fierce animal, especially if confronted on land rather than in the water.

pp. 80–81 A COOL SMOOTHIE!

Seals and sea lions have streamlined bodies to help them swim and dive and a good layer of blubber that means they can stay underwater for long periods (in some species for over an hour) without feeling the chill.

ATTITUDE

pp. 82–85 LOOKING ON THE BRIGHT SIDE

The bottlenose dolphin on pages 82–83 is playing in the warm waters of the Caribbean with its mouth open wide in what looks like a cheery grin. Dolphins live in large social groups and exhibit a great sense of fun in the way they react to and co-operate with each other.

OPPOSITE AND BELOW HAVING A WHALE OF A TIME

Whales — including the beluga or white whale below and the grey whale on the next page — like to push themselves up out of the water vertically so that they can see around them. This is known as spy hopping. Other exuberant whale behavior includes spouting water from the tops of their heads, boat bumping, tail slapping, and singing.

pp. 88–89   ELEGANT EGRET

The little egret, a small white heron with head plumes, jet black beak and legs, and yellow feet, feeds on fish which it sometimes spears with its sharp beak.

OPPOSITE   DANGEROUS DIVER

The kingfisher sits patiently above rivers and streams until it spots a victim. Then it plunges down into the water and grabs its prey.

BELOW   AN UNKNOWN QUANTITY

Although the Sardinian warbler is a common bird in Greece, Italy, and the rest of the Mediterranean, little is known about its habits. The male has a black-topped head with brown eyes surrounded by red skin.

OPPOSITE COOL HAIRDO

Demoiselle cranes are pale blue and grey. They are easily recognizable for the white plume that extends from behind their eyes well down their necks. The smallest of the cranes, they live in many parts of the world. Despite their size, they will vigorously defend their nests.

ABOVE SMALL BRAIN, GREAT MEMORY

Every year the tiny Clark's nutcracker hides thousands of seeds in different places but it can always remember where they are when it gets hungry.

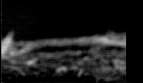

pp. 94–95 A BIT OF A PARTY ANIMAL

Flamingos are highly sociable birds, living in vast colonies and often moving as a synchronized group. They may open their wings simultaneously and lift and turn their heads at the same time, in exactly the same way.

AN EYE ON THE MAIN CHANCE

All birds of prey, including the peregrine falcon, have excellent eyesight. They can see about four times as much detail as a human and so can spot prey at a great distance. The peregrine falcon also holds an important record — it is the fastest animal alive

OPPOSITE FORWARD LOOKING ... AND WISE?

Their wisdom may belong in fairy tales, but owls certainly look straight ahead, with their huge eyes facing forward from their round faces rather than being set on each side of an angular face as with other birds. This is a great grey owl.

ABOVE AN ALERT NIGHT BIRD

Most owls are nocturnal and nothing escapes them. Their eyesight works as well in the dark as in the light and they have exceptionally good hearing.

SPECIALLY ADAPTED FOR FISHING

Ospreys are fish hawks that hunt by flying over the
water looking for fish. They hover above the surface,
before plunging in, feet-first. Ospreys usually hunt
alone in the early morning and late afternoon.
They are well adapted to their fishing lifestyles with
three toes and a thumb on each foot; the thumb
can swivel around to grasp a slippery fish more
easily. Their hooked beaks are well suited
to tearing the flesh of their victims.

ATTITUDE

pp. 106–107 PURE AGGRESSION

Great white shark in attack mode near Dyer Island in South Africa. Great whites are notoriously ferocious predators that hunt by ambushing their prey from below. They have a strong sense of smell and the scent of blood in the water can trigger a killing frenzy.

A WARY OUTLOOK

This queen angelfish from the tropical waters of the Bahamas in the Caribbean Sea, has to keep a permanent look-out for predatory fish.

OPPOSITE   A POSITIVE ATTITUDE

This delighted-looking emerald snake relishes the idea of a good supper and a chameleon might well serve the purpose. Many snakes can open their jaws incredibly wide and some boa constrictors can even dislocate them to swallow large prey.

BELOW   ROWS OF EYES

Close-up of a horsefly's face. These hairy insects are among the largest flies in the world. They have large, brightly colored compound eyes.

Lizards have every right
to be proud of
themselves. They are the
most successful group of
reptiles in the world and
can be found in almost
all habitats except
Antarctica.

A COURAGEOUS STANCE

When confronted by
a potential predator,
such as a bird of prey
or a snake, the bearded
lizard of Australia
(sometimes called a
bearded dragon),
can make an impressive
threat display by raising
its throat frill and
opening its
mouth wide.

This ornate box turtle
from the United States
has retracted into its
shell for greater
security and is certainly
not about to invite
guests home.

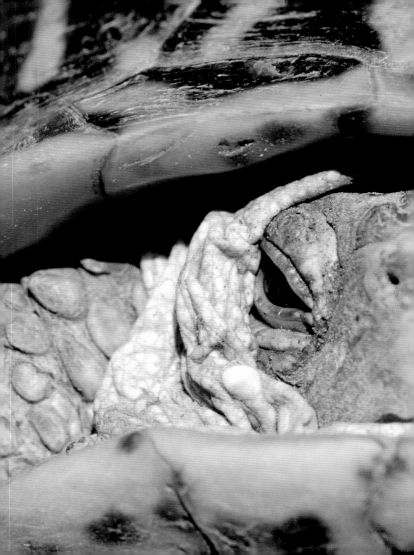

This chapter is a portrait gallery, with page after page of faces and expressions. Some animals, mainly among the primates, use facial expressions to communicate with each other. For example, chimpanzees often give toothy "fear grins" when they are frightened or trying to appease a higher-ranking individual. This may be the origin

HEADS & FACES

of the human smile, since the signal is friendly and means "I'll cooperate." Beyond conscious signalling, an animal's head, including the position of it's ears, whether it's mouth is open or closed, and the expression in its eyes, can tell us a lot about how the animal is feeling.

Alpacas may have a head for heights, but this one might have trouble seeing where it is going in its homelands high in the Andes mountains of Bolivia!

OPPOSITE   FACING UP TO THINGS

The vibrant facial color of a male douc langur, an endangered species of monkey that lives in Vietnam.

BELOW   GODLIKE

The ancient Egyptian god Anubis was generally depicted with a dog or jackal head but the prominent muzzle of this Anubis baboon would have been equally fitting.

HEADS & FACES

Black-and-white ruffed lemurs live on the island of Madagascar. Their huge eyes give them an endearing expression. These creatures are more primitive than monkeys and their large eyes (with a crystalline layer behind the retina) reflect light and provide excellent night vision.

TO BE OR NOT TO BE

With their high foreheads reminiscent of William Shakespeare, gorillas can have very soulful expressions. The males, especially, have a tall bony head crest. Their expressive facial features can reveal the animals' feelings but they can also seem pensive or even inscrutable.

REDHEADS

A curious female orangutan from Sumatra, Indonesia, gazes into the camera with a gentle expression on her face. Males have larger cheek pads and a long beard and moustache.

Profile of a koala eating eucalyptus leaves, showing its whiskered ears and bear-like muzzle. The beguiling, placid expression is not to be trusted; a koala will scratch or bite if threatened.

GETTING AN EARFUL

A greater kudu calf from Botswana. Its enormous red-tinged ears provide excellent hearing and can easily detect approaching danger.

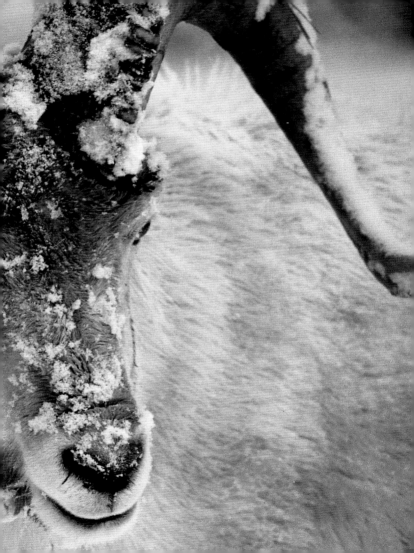

The American bighorn a is mountain sheep. Its enormous horns can weigh as much as the total weight of the rest of its skeleton.

BELOW SHEDDING VELVET

In fall, just before the rutting season, moose bulls shed the velvet covering on their antlers. They rub their antlers against shrubs and saplings and even — as this bull is doing — pull the velvet off themselves.

OPPOSITE MAGNIFICENT MALES

The impressive antlers of the male red deer have multiple points covered in velvet. They are used for battling and claiming supremacy during rutting

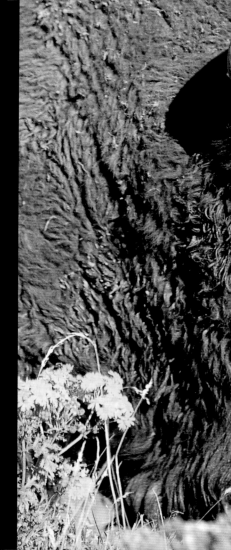

GRAZING MIGRATORS

American bison used to roam the
plains of North America in great herds,
making annual migrations of hundreds
of miles. They once numbered more
than 50 million, but are now almost
extinct in the wild. Native Americans
prized their great skulls and would
collect and decorate the bare bones.

OPPOSITE   A NOBLE FACE

The beautiful Arab is the aristocrat of the horse family.
It has a distinctive small, concave head with a slender
muzzle and large luminous eyes.

BELOW   DON'T FENCE ME IN

With its mischievous expression, this guanaco looks as if it is ready for fun.
This South American mammal is part of the camel family. The wild ancestor
of the domesticated llama and alpaca, it is adapted to life in the high altitudes
and difficult terrain of the Andes.

the intent gaze of a grey wolf. These ancestors of the domestic dog vary in color from almost white in the Arctic to yellowish brown and sometimes almost black further south.

OPPOSITE WILD DOGS

African wild dogs have short sturdy muzzles and huge ears. They hunt in packs in the early morning or evening or on bright moonlit nights.

BELOW PEEPING MARTEN

The beech marten has white fur on its neck that makes it look as if it's tucked its napkin in its collar ready to enjoy supper — which could consist of small animals, fruit or the result of a quick scavenge in human refuse bins or dumps. This marten is peeping out of its tree-trunk home.

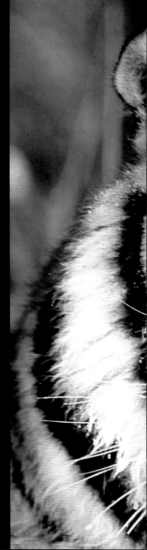

王

THE MARK OF THE KING

No two tigers have the same pattern of stripes. Siberian tigers like this one have fewer stripes than other species of tiger (about 100–150 per animal) and the stripes are broader and lighter too. Some tigers' heads appear to show the Chinese mark of "wang," or king (above), on their foreheads.

OPPOSITE   READY FOR ANYTHING

This leopard looks regal and serene, calm in the knowledge that the powerful muscles in its jaws, shoulders and forelimbs mean that it is well equipped for the kill when it does stir into action.

BELOW   THE LAST OF THE FREE

The Amur leopard of Siberia, Manchuria, and Korea, is high on the list of endangered species. Only about 50 individuals are believed to be left in the wild. Strong and elegant, its beautiful skin changes from pale yellow in winter to a reddish hue in the summer.

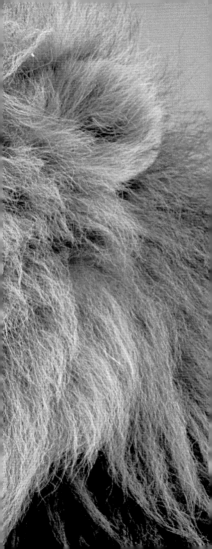

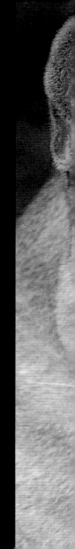

untain
ety of
ost
of the
e.

OPPOSITE BRISTLY SNOUTS

The wild boar has a dark coat of dense bristly hair plus
a long quivering snout that is very useful for foraging,
digging up bulbs and tubers, or finding nuts and insect larvae.
Males have prominent tusks.

BELOW NATURE'S BANDIT

The raccoon has a distinctive "bandit's mask" across the eyes and thick grey or almost black
fur. This creature is certainly an opportunist so its pirate-like appearance is very apt.

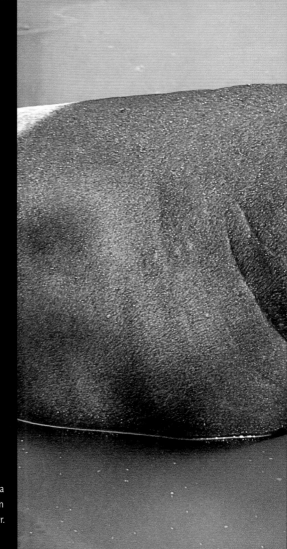

AN ALL-PURPOSE SNOUT

The tapir's snout and
upper lip form a short
mobile trunk. It uses this
trunk to pick up and eat a
wide variety of vegetation
from both land and water.

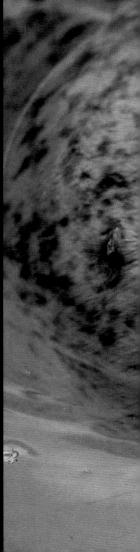

The Californian sea lion is known for its intelligence and willingness to play. This individual displays its flamboyant whiskers and avid curiosity.

OPPOSITE SOCIABLE SEALS

Huge melting eyes and bristly whiskers add to the appeal of a harbor seal as it seems to rest its muzzle on the surface of the water. These very social animals live in large groups.

ABOVE SOUTHERN SEALS

Leopard seals live in the Southern Ocean. They are unique for their elongated heads and their attacks on other seals.

The roseate spoonbill uses its big beak to extract tasty morsels from water and mud. The broad flat tip acts just like a spoon.

BELOW   WITH KNOBS ON

The male swan has a bright orange bill and, in the case of this mute swan, a distinct "knob" on the top of its beak.

OPPOSITE   HEAD OF A NATION

The regal profile of the bald eagle has been adopted
by many different groups as a symbol, including —
since 1782 — the United States of America.
The bird's name is a misnomer as it is not bald
at all but has a fine white-feathered head.

BELOW   BIRD OF THE BROAD AND SWEEPING WING

The vast golden eagle, with a wingspan of up to 7 feet
(2 m), has gold feathers on its crown and nape but its
main plumage is a rich dark brown.

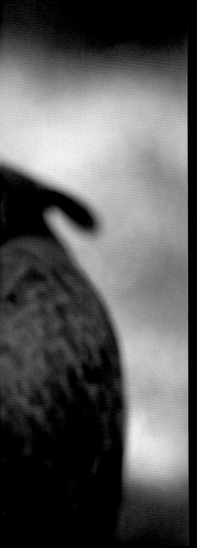

MAKING A CLEAN NECK OF IT

At first glance, the long neck of the griffon
vulture may appear to be bald but it is, in fact,
covered with fine down. This helps the bird
to avoid getting too messy when digging
into a carcass.

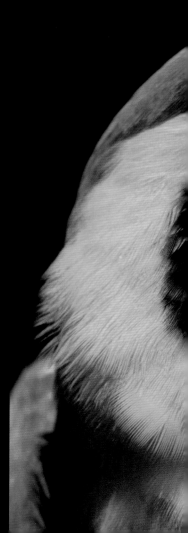

BRIGHT AND BEAUTIFUL

The blue and yellow macaw is easy to train and is probably the most intelligent parrot in the world. With its stunning plumage, it is also among the most beautiful. The blue and yellow macaw is bright green on the top of its head and then blue on its back and yellow on its belly. It has white around the eyes and a black chin.

The brown pelican has a long grey beak with a large pouch of skin that can hold up to 3 gallons (12 liters) of water and fish.

BELOW   DRESSED FOR SPRING

The squacco heron's normally yellow beak turns cobalt blue during the spring breeding season. The plumage on its back turns bright orange and the tuft of feathers on its head becomes even more prominent.

OPPOSITE KEEPING AN EYE ON THINGS

With their long necks and large eyes, ostriches scan the horizon for approaching danger. Their eyes, larger than those of any other land animal, can measure up to 2 inches (5 cm) across.

BELOW TOP NOTCH

The cassowary of Australia and New Guinea has a brightly colored blue neck and a prominent horny "helmet" which can help it carve a route though the dense rainforest vegetation in which it lives.

The rare Victoria crowned pigeon has a superb crested fan of feathers. Found in New Guinea and nearby islands, the fine "halo" of long feathers has, sadly, made it a target for collectors.

BELOW CARE TO DANCE?

The crowned crane has a crown of stiff golden feathers. Like all cranes, these African birds often engage in dancing which involves bowing, bobbing of the head, the flapping of wings, running, jumping, and throwing objects.

The great grey owl has a large round face with piercing yellow eyes and a sharp beak. The largest of the North American owls, it hunts from dusk to dawn, feeding on small animals such as voles, mice, squirrels, rabbits, frogs, and pocket gophers.

BELOW   WHITE TERROR OF THE NORTH

The speckled white snowy owl lives in the Arctic tundra and goes by many names, including ghost owl, tundra ghost, ookpik, and the white terror of the north.

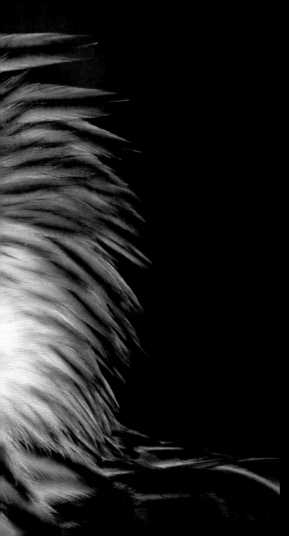

NATIONAL BIRD
OF THE PHILIPPINES

The Philippine, or
monkey-eating eagle,
is a large bird of prey
that lives in the
rainforests of the
Philippines. It is highly
endangered; some
even claim that it is
extinct in the wild.
True to its name, it
does eat monkeys
(and other small
animals), snatching
them by sweeping
down between the
trees and then
grasping them with
its huge talons.

A female king vulture that inhabits Central and South America. These birds have amazing colors and patterns on their featherless heads with beady button-like eyes.

OPPOSITE SPEED FREAKS

Head of a gannet showing the distinctive markings of the beak and eyes. A gannet's skull is especially adapted to its speed-dive style of hunting with lots of air spaces to help cushion the impact as it breaks the surface of the water. Bony flaps cover its nostril openings so that water cannot rush inside.

BELOW NIGHT FLIGHT

Swallow-tailed gulls have very distinctive red eye rings. The only nocturnal gulls in the world, they hunt at night probably using echolocation to find prey.

pp. 184–185 POWERFUL BILLS

The magnificent profile of a Stellar's sea eagle. These very large, east Asian eagles have massive, strongly arched beaks.

pp. 186–187 NOW YOU SEE ME NOW YOU DON'T

Grass snakes are among the most common snakes in Europe but their coloring provides excellent camouflage and they are not seen as often they might be.

OPPOSITE A HEAD START

The Yemen chameleon has a large bump, or casque, on the top of its head.

BELOW STAY AWAY

A leaf tailed gecko in defense mode in Madagascar shows its bright scarlet tongue and throat to ward off any unwanted visitors.

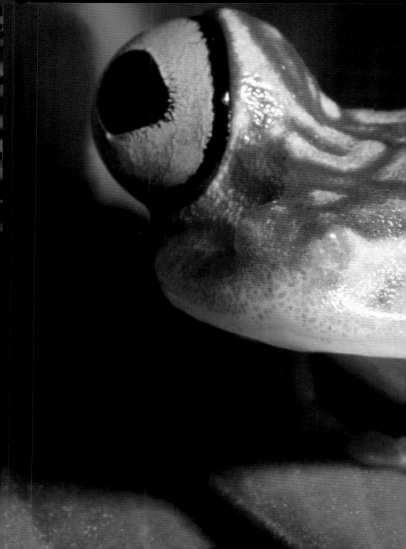

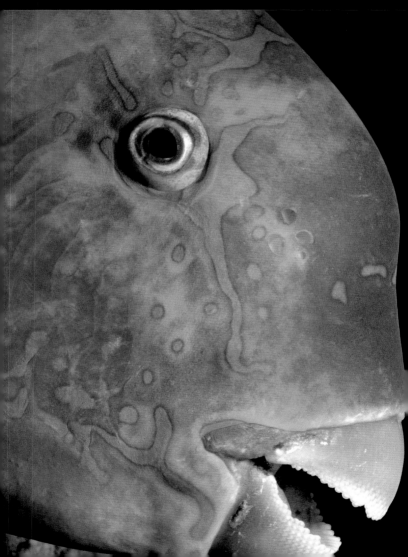

pp. 190–191 ALL THE BETTER TO SEE YOU WITH

This rainforest tree frog poses for its portrait on a leaf in Ecuador. Its large protruding eyes are enormous in proportion to the rest of its body.

pp. 192–193 THIN SKINNED

The giant Titicaca lake frog lives in Bolivia and Peru. This frog can exist happily in the cold lake waters that are starved of oxygen. It has small lungs but absorbs most of the oxygen it needs through its skin.

OPPOSITE PARROTFISH

The Pacific steephead parrotfish from Australia's Great Barrier reef is so-named because it has a sharp-edged mouth that looks just like a parrot's bill.

BELOW ORANGE ANGEL

The vibrant orange Garibaldi fish from California's Channel Islands is a busy predator and not nearly as angelic as it appears here.

pp. 196–197 A JAWFUL OF TEETH

The fearsome great white shark has several rows of razor-sharp teeth for slashing flesh. If a tooth is knocked out, a new one quickly grows in its place.

OPPOSITE DRAGONS OF THE SEA

The leafy (or weedy) sea dragon is a strange-looking seahorse that is well disguised among the weeds and plants on reefs although sometimes its bright colors are a give-away.

BELOW TIME TO PRAY

The praying mantis has huge, forward-facing eyes. It is the only insect that can swivel its head around to look behind it. This helps it to keep a look-out for passing prey.

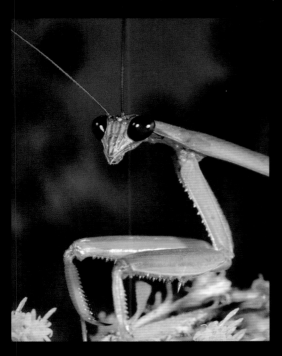

Every part of an animal's body is perfectly suited to its habitat and lifestyle. Coloring, whether of feathers, fur, scales, or skin, is designed to help the animal stay safe from predators, usually by helping it blend in with the natural colors of its surroundings. This is why, for example, polar bears are creamy white, whereas tropical birds are often a brilliant cascade of color, like the

DETAILS

rainforests they inhabit. But skin color can also carry warnings, like the poison-arrow frogs of South America who advertise their venomous skins with the brightest of hues. Specific parts of the body are often adapted to finding food (a pelican's beak), surviving in a hostile climate (thick winter coats), or attracting a mate (a peacock's tail). Whatever it takes!

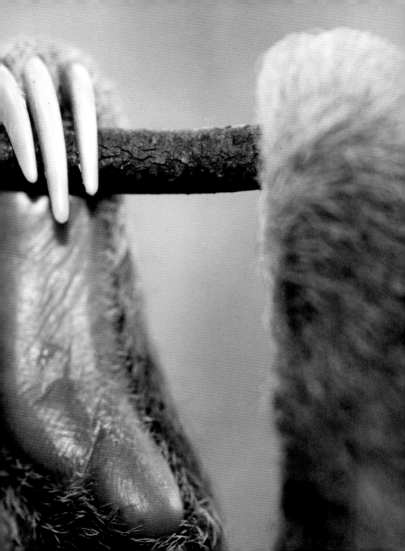

the brilliant feathers of a scarlet macaw. A bird's feathers are made from keratin, the same material that is used to make reptile scales and mammal hair.

p. 202–203 HANGING ON BY ITS TOES

The limbs and claws of a Hoffmann's two-toed sloth, native to South America. The front limb has two hooked claws at the end and the back limbs have three claws each.

OPPOSITE FANCY FOOTWORK

This is the foot of an Alpine marmot from Austria. Marmots sometimes wrestle for hours, standing on their back feet and trying to push each other over. They even eat standing up on their sturdy back feet, gripping their food with their front feet. The strong claws are especially useful when digging out their burrows.

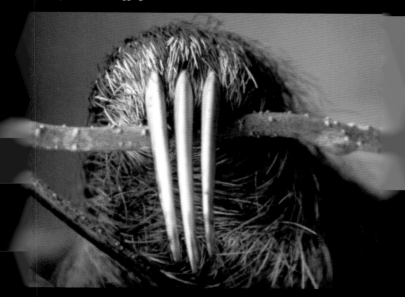

ABOVE GETTING A GRIP ON THINGS

The three toes of a brown-throated sloth, in Costa Rica.

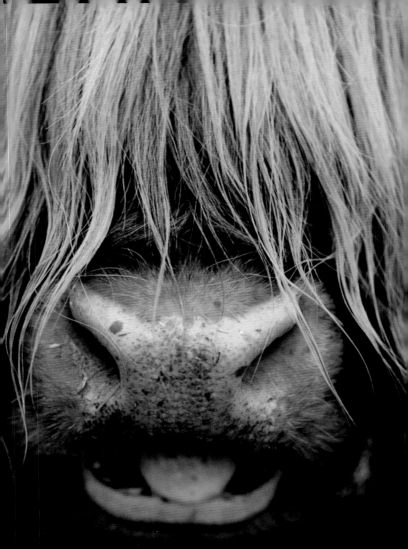

The coarse russet hair of highland cattle helps to protect them
from the freezing winter winds and snow. Hailing from the rugged
hillsides of the Scottish Highlands, this is one of the oldest — and
hardiest — breeds of cattle in the world.

BELOW   MOOSE MUZZLE

The nose and nostrils of a male moose. This animal, the largest of the deer family,
is known as an elk in Europe and a moose or wapiti in America. It has a long nose
and a drooping lip.

The horns of sheep, goats and deer serve as emblems of masculinity in the breeding season when they take the brunt of the power struggles. Horns can be long or short, straight or curved, ridged or smooth.

OPPOSITE ALL-PURPOSE TRUNK

Close-up of the trunk of an African elephant bull. The elephant's wrinkled, agile trunk can be an amazingly precise tool. It has thousands of pairs of muscles and is capable of many movements. An elephant uses its trunk to pluck grass and leaves to eat, to squirt water for drinking and washing, and to spray dust onto its hide for a dust bath.

BELOW HANDY TUSKS

An African elephant from Chobe in Botswana has strong curved tusks. The tusks of the males are especially chunky and thick. They sometimes use them to dig in the soil when looking for useful minerals, such as salt.

FEET AND TOES

Close-up view of an Indian
elephant's foot, in Thailand. Its
great legs, like the stout pillars
in an ancient church, have to
support a huge weight of about
10 ton. As all old elephant trackers
know, the circumference of an
elephant's forefoot measures about
half its height at the shoulder.

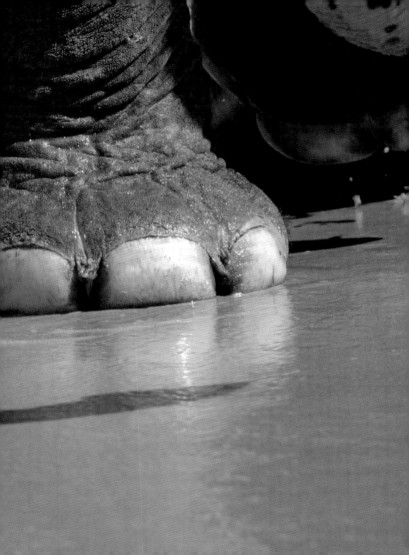

This swirl of prickly spines is a curled-up hedgehog. Baby hedgehogs are ... smooth skins but new little spines appear within a few hours of birth.

OPPOSITE FANCY STRIPES

The Grevy's zebra is the largest of all the zebras and now an endangered ... narrower and more numerous stripes than a common zebra, which has ... A mountain zebra has about 50 stripes, with three horizontal bands ne...

BELOW HAIRY HORNS

A giraffe's head with its blunt "horns." Not really horns at all, these are b... skull covered with skin and hair and are not shed. Male giraffes usually ... than females and may use them to fight, so the hair is sometimes rubbe...

COAT OF MANY COLORS

The several subspecies of giraffe are largely distinguished by the markings on their coats. But even within a subspecies, each individual has its own unique pattern. Scientists in the field often photograph the patterns on the neck and use them to identify and monitor individual giraffes, in much the same way that we use fingerprints. This giraffe has a beautiful pattern of dark brown angular patches divided by white lines.

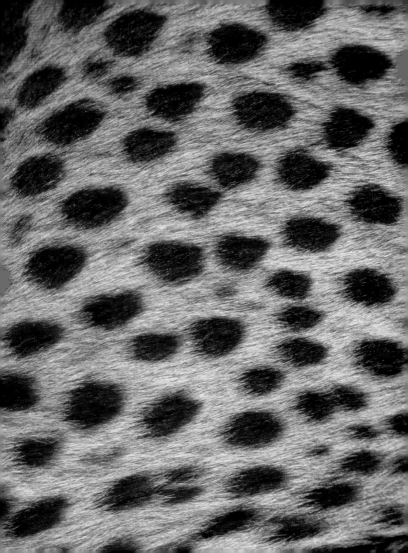

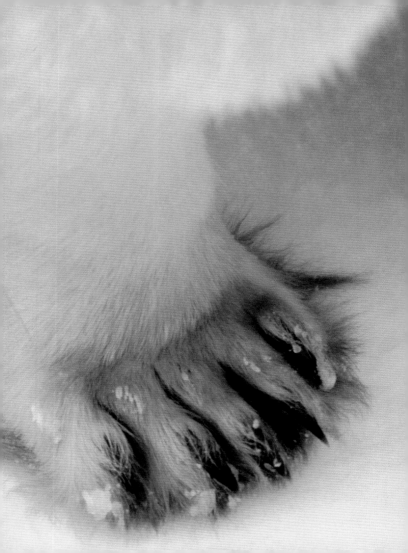

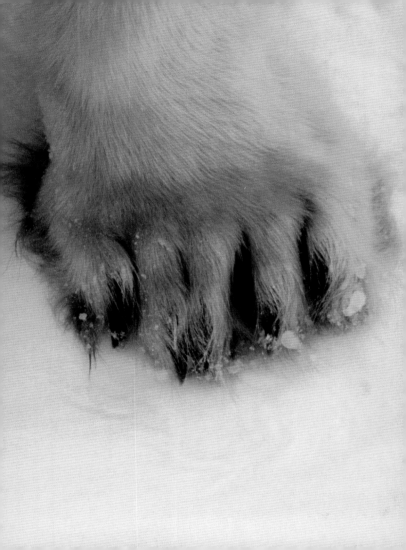

pp. 220–221 CHEETAH SPOTS

A cheetah's fur is yellowish brown with
black spots and may grow paler on its
belly. Cheetahs that live in desert
conditions usually have smaller spots.
The fur of the elegant king cheetah
(page 220) has the largest spots of all.

pp. 222–223 SNOW SHOES

This close-up view of the paws of a polar
bear shows its fearsome claws. A polar
bear's wide feet act like snow shoes,
spreading and distributing its weight so
that it does not sink into the soft snow.

OPPOSITE TOOTHWALKERS

The muzzle of a walrus on Round Island, Alaska, shows its thick
white tusks which can be over 3 feet (1 m) long on a mature male.
These large animals are cumbersome on land and they often use
their tusks (which are really just elongated teeth) to drag
themselves along.

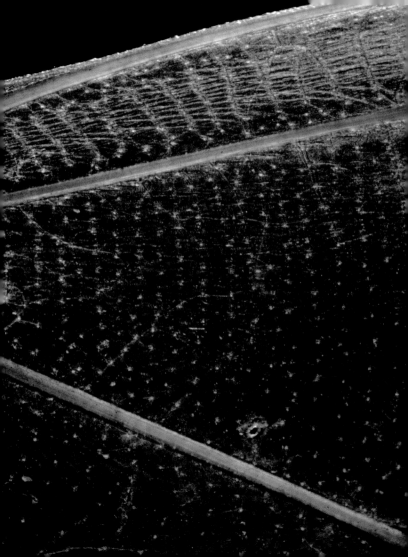

pp. 226–227   THE TAIL END

The beautiful patterns on the striped tail of an armadillo disappear into its armor-plated body.

pp. 228–229   BAT FINGERS

This looks like an autumn leaf but is, in fact, the wing membrane and arm joints of a slit faced bat from Kenya in East Africa. Bats wings are made of a double layer of skin stretched, on each side, over four very long fingers.

OPPOSITE AND BELOW   PHEASANT FINERY

The coppery underpart of the pheasant has fine dark markings and there is often a white collar. The plumage of the male pheasant varies from one subspecies to another (of which there are many), but is always a brilliant mix of colors and intricate patterns.

DETAILS

An American flamingo preens its beautiful salmon-colored feathers. Their pink color is derived from the shrimps and algae they eat — the carotenoid pigments act as a sort of dye. The colors vary from the brightest crimson or vermilion to pale pink and there is no difference in color between male and females feathers. A newly-hatched chick is grey or white and it will be one or two years before it assumes full adult coloration.

OPPOSITE COLORFUL FEATHERS

Grey partridges are gamebirds in the pheasant family that are found on farmland across most of Europe and into western Asia. They have been introduced into parts of North America. From a distance these birds seem to be a drab grey-brown, but close up their feathers are a dazzling mix of chestnut, cream, brown, grey, and pale blue. Both sexes have similar coloring.

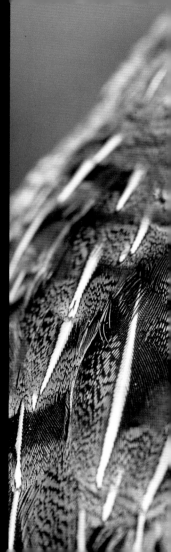

OPPOSITE   BRAGGING ABOUT IT

During courtship, the male peacock displays its extravagant shimmering tail in an arc of iridescent blue-green plumage. The colors owe their brilliance to a special optical effect called a "Bragg reflection." The magnificent tail serves no other purpose and during the rest of the year the male drags its long tail behind it.

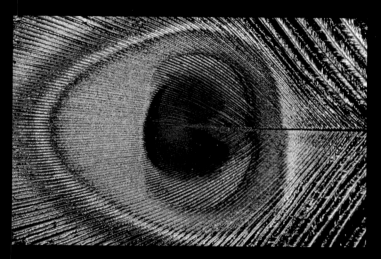

ABOVE   THE EYE OF THE BEHOLDER

An adult male peacock has about 200 feathers in its tail. Of these, about 170 have a central "eye" like the one shown here. Each year the males shed their feathers and grow new ones. Female peacocks do not have ornamental feathers but they choose their mates based on the beauty of their tails.

pp. 240–241 FLOWERY FEET

Photographed in a mangrove swamp on an island in the Galapagos chain, the feet of this red footed booby look like tropical flowers. This large seabird (part of the gannet family) breeds on islands and coasts in tropical oceans.

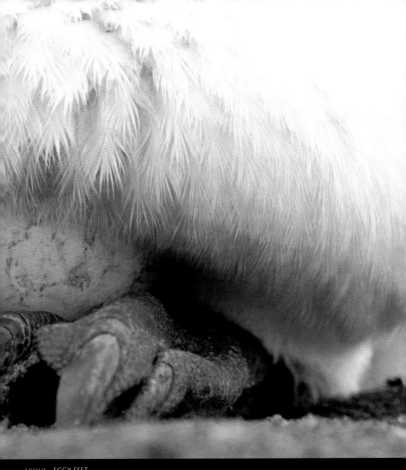

ABOVE EGGY FEET

This king penguin is holding an egg in a brood pouch on its feet. Like its larger cousin, the emperor penguin, the male king penguin incubates a single egg but it does so during the warmer summer season when food is plentiful.

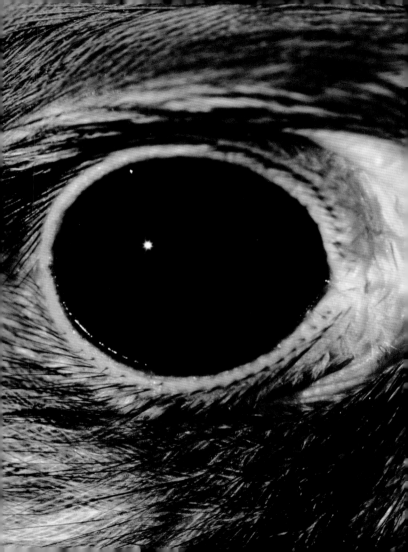

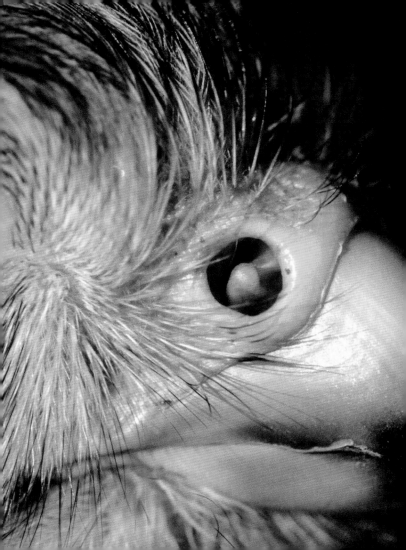

pp. 244–245   THE EYES HAVE IT

Close-up of a yellow-ringed European kestrel's eye. Kestrels use their keen eyesight to spot prey that includes small mammals such as voles, frogs, worms, small birds, and large insects.

OPPOSITE   SULAWESI HORNBILL

The crystal clear eye of a red-knobbed hornbill from the Sulawesi. These large birds have distinctive, brightly colored facial markings.

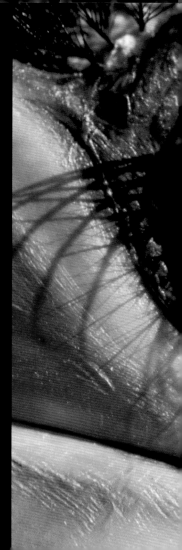

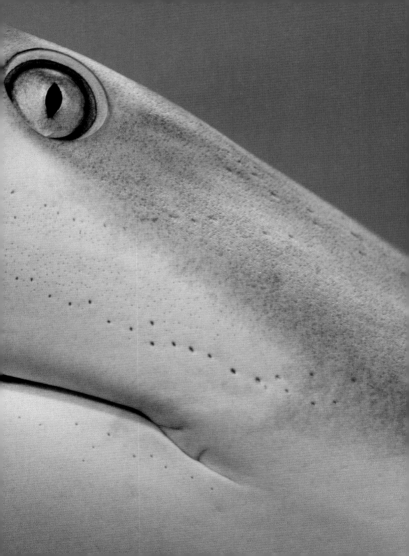

pp. 248–249 CURIOUS REEF SHARKS

A grey reef shark in the Caribbean. One of the most common sharks, it lives in the coral reefs of Indo-Pacific waters and many other places too. These curious — and sometimes dangerous — creatures have been known to swim up to scuba divers to check them out.

OPPOSITE SKIN CHANGER

A close-up view of a chameleon's skin. Chameleons are famous for being able to change color. They have special cells that lie in two layers under their transparent outer skins. The cells in the upper layer contain yellow and red pigments. The layer below is blue and white and when these cells change the animal changes color.

BELOW CALIFORNIA'S MARINE FISH

This is the brilliant orange pectoral fin of a Garibaldi fish, part of the damselfish family. This is the official marine fish of the state of California.

DETAILS

pp. 252–253 DANGEROUS FISH DISH

A close-up view of the eye of a pufferfish from the Indo Pacific. The fact that the eyes (and internal organs) of most pufferfish are highly poisonous, does not prevent them from being considered a great delicacy in Japan and Korea.

OPPOSITE   GETTING RATTLED

The jointed rattle of an Arizona black rattlesnake. Used as a warning signal, the rattle is made up of a series of hollow beads that are actually modified scales from the tail-tip. Each time the snake sheds its skin, a new rattle segment is added.

BELOW   ALLIGATOR SKIN

An alligator's skin is darker than a crocodile's hide and is often nearly black. Alligators have horny skin scales and thick bony plates with raised ridges along the back.

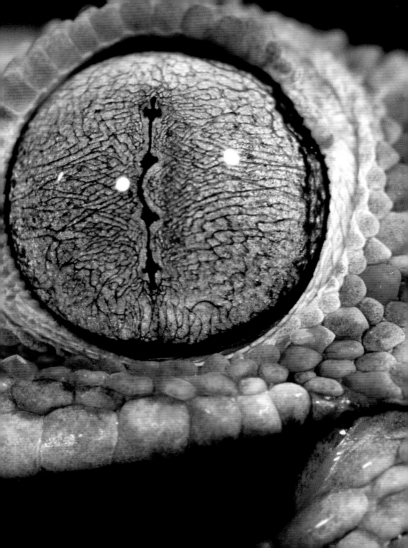

pp. 256–257 REPTILIAN VISITORS

The bright eye of a Tokay gecko from Asia. This nocturnal creature normally lives in the rainforest but sometimes enters houses, roaming about in search of insects or mice.

pp. 260–261 MANY A MOTH

Moths are incredibly numerous: about 140,000 species have been found. Their wings are actually transparent; it is their iridescent overlapping scales that gives them their color.

OPPOSITE 1,600 SUCKERS

The suckers of a giant Pacific octopus, the largest octopus in the world. The arms of the largest one ever caught (weighing in at about 600 pounds or 270 kg) spanned almost 33 feet (10 m). This species has two rows of suckers per arm and up to 1,600 suckers in all.

BELOW CRABBY VELVET

The velvet swimming crab has bright red eyes. Its carapace has a very fine covering of hair giving it the velvety texture for which it is named.

What distinguishes animals from plants and inanimate objects is their ability to move. Some animals roam far and wide: the Arctic tern, for example, flies some 16,000 miles (26,000 km) from the North Pole to the South Pole and back again every year. Wild cats, such as the mountain lion, patrol large territories, keeping unwanted intruders out. Many animals can move at great

MOTION

speed, usually in an effort to catch prey or to escape from predators. A few creatures, including the aptly named sloth, barely move at all. Its well camouflaged coat and almost imperceptible movement make it hard for predators to spot among the leaves. Some animals, such as the exuberant dolphin, appear to take great pleasure in their movement, leaping vigorously from the waves apparently just for the pure joy of it all.

Two bottlenose dolphins leap out of the blue waters of the Caribbean to sail through the air in a perfectly synchronized formation.

OPPOSITE AND BELOW   CAREFUL CHOREOGRAPHY

Sifakas are a type of prosimian that live only on the island of Madagascar. They have a unique way of moving when crossing open ground: they skip along on their hind legs with their front legs raised for balance. The effect is comical as they look like dancers performing some carefully choreographied dance.

pp. 266–267 A SPECTACULAR AFRICAN JOURNEY

Huge herds of wildebeest spend the wet season on the Serengeti plains, in Tanzania.
But toward the end of May, when the dry season begins, they form long columns and
journey north to the Masai Mara plains of southern Kenya. It is a spectacular sight to see
the tens of thousands of wildebeest migrating together. Part of the journey involves crossing
the Mara River; in this photograph a juvenile wildebeest makes a fairly daring leap.

ABOVE AND OPPOSITE FLEET FOOTED

The graceful impala antelope lives in the open woodlands and savannas of southern Africa, as far north as Kenya. These antelopes live in small, single sex herds and spend most of their time grazing and browsing on grasses, leaves, and fruit. Like all antelopes, they need to be fast runners to escape from the swift predators of the savanna. They can move at speeds of up to 55 miles (90 km) per hour, making leaps of over 33 feet (10 m) in a single bound.

MOTION

A baby African elephant out for a stroll in Samburu, Kenya. With the help of its mother, a newborn calf struggles to its feet within 30 minutes of birth. An adult elephant, walking at a normal pace, moves at about 2 to 4 miles (3 to 6 km) an hour but can reach 24 miles (40 km) an hour at full speed.

BELOW LONG LIMBS FOR SPEED AND DEFENSE

A giraffe stands tall on front legs that appear to be much longer than its hind legs; in fact, they measure only 10 percent more. These long limbs mean that giraffes can run swiftly. They are also useful weapons of defense against predators who venture too close.

pp. 272–273 ANDALUSIAN ELEGANCE

A grey Andalusian stallion at the gallop in Colorado. The ancient Andalusian breed, originally from Spain, is renown for its speed and the elegance of its gait.

pp. 274–275 AN AGILE AMERICAN CAT

A young puma, or mountain lion, chasing prey through a mountain stream. Pumas can move at speeds of up to 30 miles (50 km) an hour, jump 20 feet (6 m) from a standing position, and leap vertically 8 feet (2.5 m). These solitary cats often patrol a territory of some 100 square miles (260 sq km).

HOP TO IT

Kangaroos are unique in being the only large animals that move by hopping. They generally hop along at about 12 miles (20 km) an hour, although they can reach speeds of 40 miles (70 km) an hour over short distances.

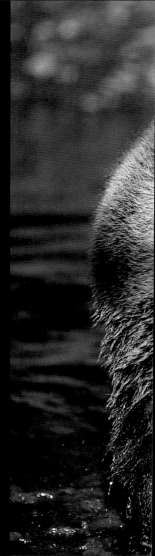

A wild boar trots along in Tuscany, Italy. These woodland animals can move surprisingly quickly and are also good swimmers. The wild boar is the largest of the wild pigs. The ancestor of the domestic pig, it is native to the woodlands of Europe, North Africa, and parts of Asia. It has also been introduced to the southern United States and New Zealand.

AGILE FISHERS

Brown bears are generally solitary animals, although on the western seaboard of North America they gather together by streams and rivers to catch salmon returning upstream to spawn. They are agile fishers, grabbing salmon from the rushing waters and gobbling them up.

OPPOSITE ARCTIC DRIFTERS

A polar bear striding out over the crisp snow. Polar bears make long journeys, but not necessarily on foot. They live mainly on sea ice and can travel thousands of miles on the drifting ice.

BELOW COOL SWIMMERS

A polar bear swimming in Canada. Polar bears are strong swimmers and can often be seen in open waters many miles from land. They spend a lot of time in the water hunting seals. They use their large forepaws to paddle along at up to 6 miles (10 km) per hour.

MOTION

pp. 284–285 FAST WHITE WOLF

Arctic wolves are a subspecies of the grey wolf. They are slightly smaller than their southern cousins and live in small packs of just a few animals. They are swift moving predators.

OPPOSITE NOW WHICH WAY?

A European otter poised on a river bank looks about, perhaps for food. River otters move swiftly in search of fish, frogs, crayfish, and crabs. They eat about 15 percent of their body weight every day.

BELOW IT'S EASY. LOOK NO HANDS!

Sea otters often float along on their backs. Unlike seals or whales, otters do not have a layer of insulating blubber, but a dense layer of soft fur protected by an outer layer of long guard hairs that keeps them warm in the water. Their slim, streamlined bodies move through the water gracefully, propelled by the action of their webbed paws.

OPPOSITE UNDERWATER MONKS

Hawaiian monk seal swimming underwater. These seals spend many days at sea before returning to land where they come ashore on sandy beaches to escape sharks or simply to rest while they digest their food. Monk seals are an endangered species and it is believed that only about 1,400 Hawaiian monk seals exist today.

ABOVE ESCAPING UNWANTED ATTENTION

This female grey seal is running along a beach to escape the attentions of a male. The grey seal breeds in several colonies on and around coasts. This is the largest native mammal in the British Isles, with the bulls reaching over 9 feet (3 m) long. The cows are smaller, usually up to 6 feet 6 inches (2 m) long.

pp. 290–291 UNIQUE MAMMAL

A platypus swimming underwater in Australia. This strange creature has webbed feet that propel it through the water and a large, rubbery snout that looks like a duck's bill. On land, it moves with a reptile-like gait, having its legs set on the sides of its body, rather than underneath. The platypus is nocturnal and semi-aquatic.

AQUATIC ACROBATS

Bottlenose dolphins leaping in the Caribbean. These are the largest of the beaked dolphins and often appear in captive performances as they respond very well to training and are amazingly adaptable acrobats.

pp. 294–295 FLYING MAMMALS

Noctule bat in flight, showing its sharp fierce-looking teeth. This bat has a wing span of nearly 14 inches (35 cm) and is one of the largest bat species in Europe. It flies high and fast above the forest tree tops. Bats are the only mammals that can fly.

pp. 296–297 DANCING IN THE AIR

Two sea gulls seem to be suspended in the air with their white tail feathers fanned out like a ballerina's tutu. Their flying skills enable them to catch prey in mid-air.

WHOOPING IT UP

Whooper swans are named for their deep honking call. They breed in Iceland and Scandinavia and then migrate to the United Kingdom and Europe for the winter. The whooper is the national bird of Finland and appears on Finnish Euro coins.

OPPOSITE MOVERS AND SHAKERS

The greylag goose lives in wetlands such as lakes, marshes, and damp heather moors. It is quite a large goose, measuring some 32 inches (80 cm) long with a wingspan of over 5 feet (155 cm).

BELOW DUCKING UNDER THE SURFACE

Ruddy ducks breed in marshy lakes and ponds in many parts of North America. They can dive and swim underwater where they search for the seeds and roots of aquatic plants to eat, as well water insects and crustaceans.

OPPOSITE   THE LONGEST JOURNEY

The graceful Arctic tern makes the longest migratory
journey of any bird. Every fall, the terns leave Canada
and Greenland, ride the westerly winds across the
Atlantic Ocean, and then head south down the west
coast of Africa. They summer in the South Pacific
and then head north again as the southern winter
approaches. The round trip is about 16,000 miles
(26,000 km).

BELOW   LAGGING BEHIND

Greylag geese landing, with their red legs dangling down like an airplane's wheels in landing
mode. This goose is the ancestor of domestic geese in Europe and North America and is one
of the last species to leave when it is time to migrate. Hence some people believe that its
name derives from its tendency to "lag behind" the others.

ONE UP, ONE DOWN! Ground hornbills live on the savannas and open grasslands of sub-Saharan Africa. Although these large birds can fly, they spend most of their time on the ground, where they walk, instead of hopping along like most birds. According to some African peoples, these birds are rain prophets, while for the Masai their presence on the roof of a house signals imminent death.

MOTION

HUNTER ON THE WING

A tawny owl in flight with its chestnut brown wings raised high and shaggy "trousered" legs dangling down as it swoops from its perch to hunt.

SUNSET SOARER!

The magnificent red kite is a very agile flyer, able to tilt its long forked tail like a rudder. With a wingspan of about 6 feet (nearly 2 m) but weighing only 2–3 pounds (1–1.5 kg), it can soar in the air with hardly a wing beat for hours at a time.

pp. 310–311 WHITE IBIS SQUADRON

A small flock of white ibis with their distinctive black-tipped wings and long, curved beaks flies in tight formation. White ibis live in marshes and swamps where they use their long bills to scoop up crabs and crayfish.

pp. 312–313 SANDWICH TIME

Sandwich terns breed on sandy coastlines. Here an enormous flock swirls and wheels up above a group on the beach below. These terns are quite bulky with a short tail and no tail-streamers. Their long wings are pale with black edges.

SUNSET BOULEVARD

A languid trail of flamingos seems to loop around a glowing sunset. Flamingos live in huge flocks, often numbering hundreds of thousands of birds.

SUSPENDED ANIMATION
A broad billed hummingbird hovers while taking nectar from a flower with its long pointed beak. Hummingbirds beat their wings very quickly and need to consume up to 50 percent of their body weight in nectar every day. Because they spend so much time in the air they have poorly developed feet and can hardly walk.

pp. 318–319

EMPERORS ON ICE

A single file of Emperor penguins in the Antarctic. These birds may tramp along for over 625 miles (1,000 km) when hunting for food, especially if traveling between the nesting site and the open sea.

pp. 320–321

EMPERORS UNDERWATER

Emperor penguins are the diving champions of the birds and can descend to 1,600 feet (500 m). Humans can only go to 500 feet (150 meters) before the water pressure collapses their lungs.

SLOWLY DOES IT

A tortoise lumbers along, scrambling over any obstacles en route.

This jellyfish is a bell jelly floating along in the Pacific Ocean, off the coast of California. Most jellyfish drift along taking life as it comes, feeding on any small fish and plankton that become entangled in their tentacles.

A green turtle swimming in the Pacific Ocean, near Hawaii. This turtle grows to 5 feet (1.5 m) in length and can weigh 450 pounds (200 kg). It is the largest hard-shelled turtle. As marine animals, green turtles spend most of their lives in the sea but do come onto the beaches to lay eggs or, sometimes, just to bask on the warm sand for a while.

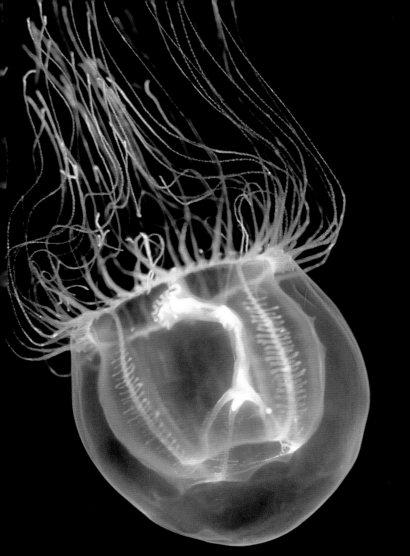

OPPOSITE   WEBBED GLIDER

Frogs have five digits on their back legs and four on their front legs. Those that spend most of their lives in water have webs of skin between these digits. Tree frogs, on the other hand, have adhesive pads on the end of each "toe" to provide better grip. The Wallace's gliding frog shown here has such extensive webbing that it can use it to glide over quite long distances.

BELOW   FALSE FLYER

The flying lizard (sometimes called a flying dragon) is a small tropical Asian lizard. It has 5 to 7 elongated ribs that act rather like an airplane's wing struts when it is gliding through the air with its outstretched "wings" of skin giving it the necessary lift. Despite its name, it doesn't actually fly, but glides instead.

This male chameleon is stalking along a slender branch in the Cameroon, Africa. It wraps its prehensile tail around the branch and digs its toes in to ensure a firm grip as it moves through the trees.

HELI-BUMBLES?

This bumblebee is flying away from a lamium flower (a spotted deadnettle). A bumblebee's wing oscillates to maintain its position in the air. In this way, the dynamics of its flight relate more closely to the way a helicopter's rotor works than to the action of an airplane wing.

Scientists are not sure what the function of sleep really is, although most agree that it gives the brain time to reorder information and "tidy up" after the activities of the day. Like humans, most animals spend a part of each day or night resting or sleeping, presumably for the same purpose.

STILLNESS AND REST

The puzzling thing is the huge variation in the amount of time the different species spend sleeping. Cats, bats, and sloths, for example, can sleep for up to 20 hours a day, while horses only need five hours and giraffes get by with just four hours each day. A very few species, such as the spider-mouse, are active 24 hours a day.

p. 333   RESTING IN PEACE

The peaceful face of a sleeping silverback mountain gorilla
in the Virunga National Park, in the Congo. Gorillas spend
the day foraging on the forest floor. At nightfall they build
a nest on the ground or up in the trees to sleep in.
They make a fresh nest each night.

OPPOSITE SLEEP FEAST

Australian koalas sleep for up to19 hours each day. They live
and sleep in eucalyptus trees where they feel comfortable
and secure and can eat the leaves; in fact, koalas eat so
many eucalyptus leaves that they smell of eucalyptus.

p. 336   SNUGGLED UP TO MOM

A crowned lemur baby is sound asleep snuggled into its mother's fur,
in Madagascar's Ankarana Special Reserve. Adult lemurs are nocturnal.
They are solitary foragers, but sleep together in small groups in the day.

p. 337   SLEEPING PEACEFULLY

A pygmy anteater resting in Guyana, South America. Its sharp curved claws are
very useful for gripping the branches when climbing — and sleeping — in trees.

OPPOSITE AND BELOW   WAKE UP, MOMMY!

Chimpanzees are active during the day. At dusk
they build individual sleeping nests in trees (see right).
They may also rest on the ground during the day,
especially the exhausted mothers of young chimps!

This male red kangaroo is resting with a white wagtail perched on its rump. Male kangaroos are called bucks, boomers, or jacks; females are does, jills, or flyers, and young ones are joeys. A group of kangaroos is called a mob.

OPPOSITE LAZY LIONS

Life is one big yawn, or so it would seem, since lions spend most of their time asleep. Actually there are good reasons for their apparent laziness. Hunting is a high energy way of obtaining food with a relatively low success rate. Lions only eat once every 2 or 3 days, when they gorge themselves. Afterward they take a good long rest, which makes the meal last longer.

ABOVE NIGHT HUNTERS

Lions are mainly nocturnal hunters. They spend the long hot days resting.

Lioness and cub sleeping, in Botswana, Africa. Adult lions sleep about 21 hours a day (that's even more than domestic cats!); cubs sleep about the same amount and spend the rest of the time playing.

OPPOSITE   LIFE AT THE TOP

Leopards spend a lot of time in the trees. They often eat up there and doze in the safety and relative cool of the branches, their relaxed legs dangling down.

BELOW   A WELL EARNED REST

Cheetahs usually hunt and eat in the late morning or early afternoon when many other large carnivores are likely to be asleep. Young cheetahs are taught to hunt by their mothers. This cub is resting after a training season.

SNOOZE

urled up snugly with the tip of its nose tucked
old, in the same position that pet dogs often
sleep in burrows in the side of a cliff or hill
ate, despite the freezing temperatures.

nd moss in hollow tree trunks, or build
es. They do not hibernate and are active
cold winter's day, they often tuck themselves
l.

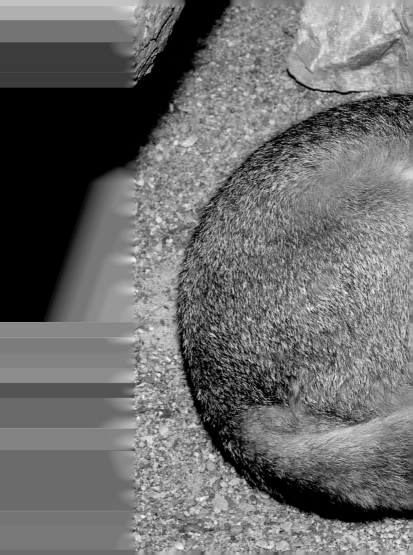

STILLNESS & REST

pp. 356–357   OUT ON A LIMB

The red (or lesser) panda rests in tree branches, where it is safe from predators. It often basks in the sunshine high in the canopy. The female makes her nest in a tree hole lined with soft plant material such as leaves and moss. This panda looks particularly relaxed with its legs slung over the branch.

OPPOSITE AND BELOW   SNOOZERS IN THE SNOW

The polar bear's immense thick coat keeps it warm when it chooses to snooze on the ice. Polar bears hibernate in dens under the snow during the winter. During this time the females give birth to two or three cubs that emerge with her in the spring. Here a mother bear rests on the ice with her cubs huddled up against her.

A grizzly bear sleeps on a rock in Alaska, with its long front claws gripping the rocks. Grizzlies use these curved claws when digging dens and searching for roots, bulbs, and rodents to eat. They can charge at speeds of over 35 miles (56 km) per hour, faster than an Olympic athlete, so they need quality resting time in order to recover from their jaunts!

OPPOSITE AND BELOW   PINNIPEDS RESTING

Seals, sea lions, and walruses are grouped together in an order called pinnipeds. Seals often leave the water at low tide to digest food and rest. Harbor seals prefer to sleep on land but may rest in the water; they have to wake up regularly to come to the surface and breathe. Harbor and elephant seals often "bottle" — keeping most of the body submerged but with their faces peeping out to breathe. Northern elephant seals may sleep deep underwater. Grey seals sleeping on land or at the surface sometimes have REM (rapid-eye-movement), so they probably dream.

Herds of hippopotamus sleep and rest in the water during the day. Sometimes they settle into lines, with their heads on their neighbors' rumps. Hippos breathe air; when asleep underwater, their ears fold over and nostril flaps shut as they submerge. The hippos remain asleep as their bodies come back to the surface and then submerge repeatedly.

OPPOSITE   CAMPING OUT

A white tent-making bat roosting in Costa Rica's Atlantic rainforest. Some bats make tents from foliage; they bite the leaf veins to make the leaves collapse and then roost under them. Only a few bats are known to make their own roosts. Generally, these are small bats that can be hidden by a single large leaf.

EYES WIDE OPEN

A Peters epauletted fruit bat, roosting in South Africa. A bat holds its forearms along the sides of its body when it is resting. Bats have 4 very long fingers and a smaller thumb on the tip of each "hand." The claw on each thumb is used for gripping when the bat is resting. Both the curved toes and claws grip tightly even when the bat is fast asleep.

These tent-making bats are settled into a palm leaf, in Panama, Central America. Usually, a single adult male bat sets up a harem of 5 to 15 females that he will defend against any challenge. Roosting groups remain together during the mating season. At other times of the year, bachelor males may roost alone in tents while females with young may have their own tents. Some harem males keep the same group for up to three years, while the females may stay together for life.

OPPOSITE RESTING ON ONE LEG

A black stork rests with one leg raised. Storks eat reptiles, shellfish, and insects as well as fish. Generally a forest species, this stork hunts in streams and small rivers, marshy ponds, and meadows.

OUT ON A LEDGE

Two puffin species live in Alaskan waters: the horned puffin and the tufted puffin. Usually tufted puffins eat and sleep out at sea but they come ashore when it is time to nest and raise their young on the steep cliffs. Tufted puffins have tufts of feathers that curl back from each side of the head.

OPPOSITE   TUCKED UP

An Emperor penguin chick sleeping in Antarctica. Emperor penguins have no predators when they are on land so can rest securely there. They sleep standing up when they are incubating an egg or protecting a chick, but often lie down on their bellies at other times. They spend the long winter nights huddled together without moving.

BELOW   SLEEPING KINGS

These king penguins are taking a nap, heads bent over to the side. King penguins are the second largest species of penguin, after Emperor penguins. They live in the northern parts of Antarctica and the islands of the Southern Ocean.

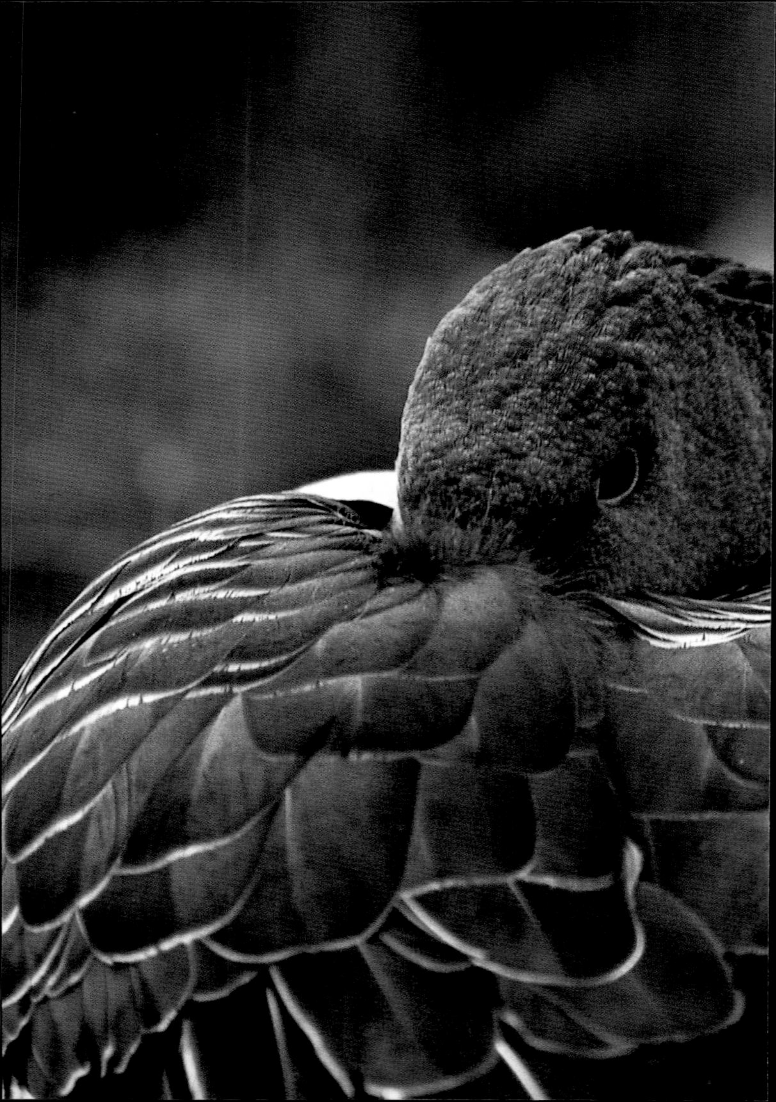

Six little bee-eaters take a rest perched
on a branch in the Masai Mara, Africa.
These brilliant little birds often perch on fences,
telegraph wires, and branches, waiting to chase
insects such as bees, wasps, and hornets.
The birds rub the insect's tail and sting
against the perch to remove the venom (and
sometimes the sting) before eating their catch.

SLEEPY HEADS

A greylag goose with its head tucked under its
wing. These birds seem able to relax and very
quickly drop into sleep mode. Hand-reared
greylag geese usually bond closely with their
owners and fit into a routine that may well
include being "put to bed" in a secure place.

STANDING GUARD

This flock of greylag geese is resting in a field. They can rest easy because one bird is keeping a watch out for predators. If it sounds the alarm the rest of the geese can be on the wing in just a few seconds.

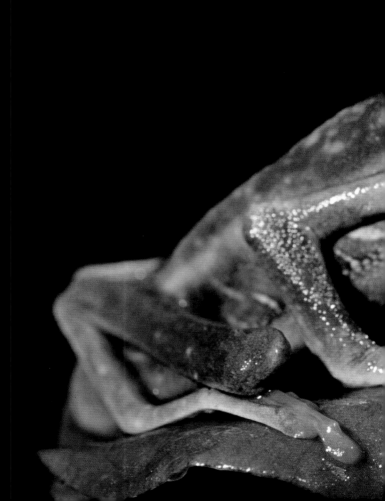

pp. 382–383   RED EYES

Red-eyed treefrogs from the rainforests of Costa Rica in Central America are nocturnal. Their red eyes help them to see when they emerge at night to search for tasty bugs to eat. Their eyes also act as a form of protection, surprising a predator when they suddenly open to show their bright red color and giving the frog a few precious seconds to escape.

OPPOSITE   CHAMELEON NAPPING

Almost half of the world's species of chameleon live in Madagascar and it has the largest chameleon community, with 59 different species that exist nowhere else. An estimated 134 chameleon species exist; eight new species of dwarf chameleons have been discovered since 1990.

BELOW   360-DEGREE VISION

A desert chameleon on the sand in Namibia. Chameleons are diurnal; they sleep at night, closing those amazing eyes that can move independently and survey the world with almost 360-degree vision.

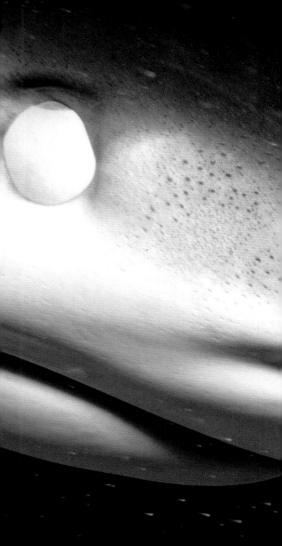

ourtship and mating are critical steps in the lif ycles of most animals. The drive to reproduce i strong instinct and there are many elaborate nd even bizarre, types of behavior associated ith breeding. Courtship rituals often begi ith males fighting to establish breeding rritories or dominance over females. A mal

FINDING
A MATE

ay also perform elaborate dances or displays repare nests or dens, or offer gifts as a nticement to allow him to mate with a femal When courtship is successful, mating follow With successful mating a new generation o nimals is produced, ready to takes its parent lace in the animal kingdom

p. 393 LOOK AT ME!

Birds display some of the most striking and elaborate courtship behaviors. The male great frigate bird swells its red throat sac up during its courtship display like a scarlet balloon. Since the birds often display together the overall effect can be stunning.

OPPOSITE   SIKA DEER

Male and female Sika deer. This species from Asia is critically endangered so successful mating is vital. During summer some males begin to mark out territory which they defend against other males. Then they round up a harem of about 12 females with which they mate.

BELOW   ROARING

A red deer stag roars during rutting. Continuous calling requires a great deal of stamina so is a good indication of the male's strength and quality as a mate.

In fall, male fallow deer mark out an area of land, known as a "stand," from which they exclude other adult males. Females and young deer stay within the male territories. As the females come into heat they are mated by the male territorial leader. After the rutting season, the males gradually lose interest in their stands and form all-male groups until the following year.

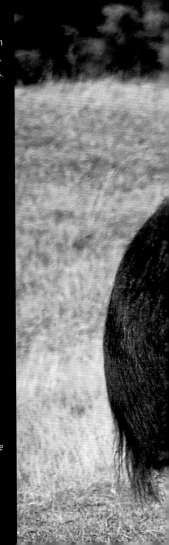

LIKE BANGING YOUR HEAD AGAINST A BRICK WALL

Male musk oxen become sexually mature at four to five years old. In the period leading up to breeding, they fight ferocious battles which involve charging at one another while bellowing and then colliding head on. The collisions can be heard from a distance and it can take up to 20 charges to decide the winner.

pp. 400–401 MALES TAKE CARE

Cape buffalos in the Masai Mara, Kenya, during courtship. The male may be nearly twice the
weight of the female so some careful manoeuvring is required during mating.

Gemsbok (or southern oryx) males fighting in Namibia. As with many desert animals,
they breed whenever conditions are favorable, all year round.

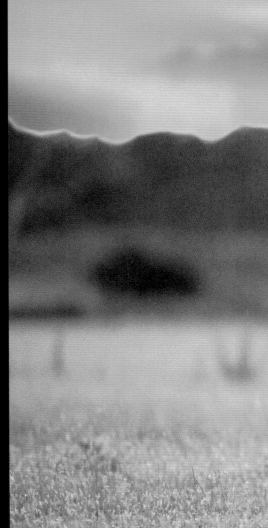

BOXING MATCH

Kangaroos live in mobs, usually led by one dominant male. During the mating season, the male leader is challenged by other males for mating rights. They fight by standing on their hind legs, often locking arms and trying to push each other over in a veritable "trial of strength." These fights are often called boxing matches.

HELLO, DARLING

Asiatic lions during courtship. They live in small prides with often just two related females and their young. During courtship, a female in heat will rub sensuously against the male.

Two male hippopotamuses fighting during courtship. These battles can last for several hours. Fighting includes clashing tusks, rearing, tussling with locked lower jaws, and biting.

OPPOSITE   BELLOWING ABOUT IT

Northern elephant seal male calling in Baja California, Mexico. The males bellow loudly and display to attract females.

BELOW   FEMALE SCENTS

This male Indian rhinoceros lifts his head, opens his mouth, and inhales deeply in what is known as the flehmen response. He is capturing female scents in the air and bringing them into contact with the Jacobsen's organ in the roof of his mouth to analyze them for hormones that will tell him if a female is willing to mate.

pp. 412–413   CUDDLING UP
A Southern elephant seal
male and a female appear
to have a warm hug during
their courtship. These
creatures live in Patagonia
and Argentina.

BOWER BUILDERS
Male bowerbirds in
northern Australia and New
Guinea construct elaborate
bowers to attract females.
In this case, a female satin
bowerbird is inspecting the
handiwork of a prospective
mate. He has not only built
the bower, but has collected
a number of blue objects
which the females of this
species find appealing.

FINDING A MATE

HANDSOME TURKEYS
Wild turkey males displaying in Texas. They spread their wings low, fan their tails, and gobble loudly to attract females' attention.

COLORFUL MALES
In the world of birds, it is often the males who sport exotic colors in order to attract the generally duller colored hens. Here a blue-black male black grouse with red eyebrows and white wing tips is watched intently by a brown-grey female.

OPPOSITE SINGING FOR A MATE

The melodious male reed warbler sings to attract a mate.
The females spend several days listening to different males before
choosing a partner. They seem to prefer the males with the largest
repertoire and the most complex melodies. This pair have gone
a step further and are preparing the nest.

BELOW BEARING GIFTS

Here a male tern is offering a small fish to a female during courtship. His ability to provide
such gifts will be some indication of his skill in providing food in the future for the female
when she must stay on the nest to care for the eggs and then the offspring.

An English pheasant cock calling; he is raised up in a cocky stance, whirring his feathers, with his brilliant colored plumage on display.

FANCY FEATHERS

Male and female Eurasian teals. The male is a veritable dandy with bright plumage during the breeding season but he will revert to a more modest style of dress by mid-summer.

SHOWING OFF

Geese during coutship. The males swim in a haughty upright posture in order to attract the females, every now and then dipping their heads into the water.

DRESSED TO KILL

Male weaver birds build nests to attract a mate. Their success depends on their appearance and the quality of the nest they build. Females fly around looking for the best built nest. Here a female red header weaver bird inspects a potential mate's work.

BELOW DO YOU LIKE MY FEATHERS?

Male birds of paradise make spectacular displays to impress prospective partners. Here a female Raggiana bird of paradise checks out a male.

pp. 428–429   A COURTSHIP DANCE

Great crested grebes during their elaborate courtship "dance" when their crests are raised and their long necks seem to sinuously dance. They also offer dangling strips of weed to each other.

OPPOSITE   A MATE FOR LIFE

Japanese cranes perform their courtship dance. These birds form lifelong partnerships and have become a symbol of good luck and happiness.

BELOW   PUFFINS IN LOVE

Puffins pair bonding in the Western Isles of Scotland. During the mating season, both males and females grow a horny covering on their beaks with handsome stripes of red, yellow, and blue.

Macaroni penguins have a golden feathered crest and a large orange-brown bill. Like all penguins, they breed in huge colonies.

OWLISH AFFECTION

Little owls perch close together during their courtship rituals (this pair is in Spain). Little owls of both sexes look alike, although the females may be larger.

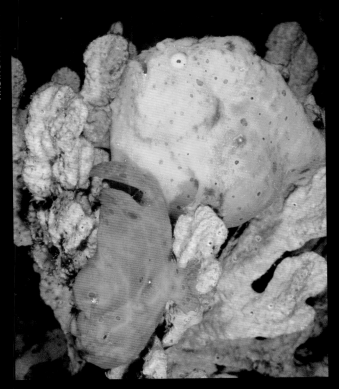

ABOVE FROGFISH LOVE

A pair of painted frogfish from Indonesia mating; the female fish is yellow.
These strange colorful creatures are related to the angler fish.

OPPOSITE MANDARINFISH

Mandarinfish mating in Indonesia, pressed close together. This strikingly colored
fish lives in coral reefs and in inshore waters.

OPPOSITE   DOES SIZE MATTER?

There is a vast difference between the sizes of these map tree frogs mating in a rainforest in Peru. Each species of frog has its own special call to attract a mate.

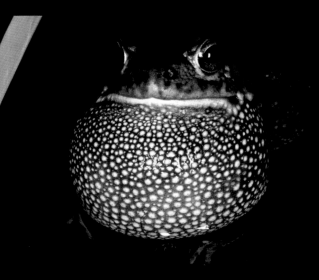

ABOVE   CALLBOYS

Frogs and toads summon the females to the mating site by croaking and calling loudly. In some species the male's throat may swell dramatically and can be vividly colored to add to the impact of the display.

pp. 440–441   DETERMINED MALES

A male flap-necked chameleon chasing a female in Zanzibar. This rather aggressive creature will hiss when angry or alarmed and may force some rival males off the tree branches before claiming the right to mate.

pp. 442–443   SCENT TRAILS

Snakes use chemical scent trails to locate each other when the time is right for mating. Here a pair of smooth snakes from Dorset, England, are coiled together to mate.

The vast majority of animals grow up without any parental care at all. Most invertebrates, fish, reptiles, and amphibians never know their parents. Their survival depends on instinct and, as they grow, experience gained by trial and error. Parental care is most prevalent among mammals and, to a lesser degree, birds, where offspring are

RAISING A FAMILY

usually born at a stage when they are unable to fend for themselves. Among birds, care begins before birth with the period of incubation, usually carried out by the female. In general, parental care is provided by the females, with some notable exceptions. Mammal babies, often born blind and bald, require the longest period of parental care.

p. 445 FEMALES IN CHARGE

A ring tailed lemur with young in Madagascar. Females stay in the group for their entire lives and dominate the social strata, while males change troops. The breeding season runs from April to June, with the female lemurs ready to mate for just for one day only. Each will have one or two offspring.

OPPOSITE GORILLA MOMS

Lowland gorilla mother and baby. These gorillas live in family groups with one dominant male, some five to seven adult females, younger family members, and sometimes a few subordinate males. The baby will share a nest with its mother and stay with her for about four years, until she has her next baby.

BELOW MARRIED FOR LIFE

A white-handed gibbon with her baby in Southeast Asia. Gibbons form monogamous pairs. The single baby will remain with the family group until it is five or six years old.

pp. 448–449 MONKEYING AROUND
These vervet monkeys are an endangered species from Africa. They live in family troops led by a dominant male and several females with their young.

pp. 450–451 HAVING A HOT BATH
A female Japanese macaque with her offspring in a hot spring in Joshin-etsu National Park, Japan. These monkeys are famous for bathing in hot springs during the cool winter months. The macaque is the only monkey native to Japan.

CARING MOTHERS
An orangutan mother with her baby in Gunung Leuser National Park, in Indonesia. The female gives birth up in the treetops and then carries her baby around in the canopy as it clings tightly to her.

An orangutan mother and baby in Indonesia. These babies are especially appealing and, sadly — despite this being illegal — many infant orangutans are captured to be sold as pets.

BELOW   AFFECTIONATE BABIES

An orangutan baby "kissing" its mother in Borneo. Orangutans care for their babies over a long period — until the youngster is about eight years old. One female observed in captivity suckled her baby for six years.

pp. 456–457 CHIMPANZEE MOTHERS

A mother chimpanzee and her baby in Gombe, Tanzania. The baby will be fed and groomed by its mother for some three to four years.

OPPOSITE SAFETY POUCH

A wallaby with her joey. Even when the joey is old enough to leave the pouch, it hops back into it when any danger threatens.

BELOW MARSUPIAL BABIES

Eastern grey kangaroo joey in its mother's pouch in Tasmania.

ABOVE WHICH ONE IS MOM?

Mother zebras keep the other members of the
herd away for three or four days until the new
foal recognizes her as its mother.

OPPOSITE UPSY DAISY

A mother zebra is nudging her newborn foal
to get it onto its feet within a few minutes
of birth. It will be another week before it
starts to graze.

OPPOSITE DELAYED BIRTH

A roe deer mother and fawn. Some European roe deer have delayed implantation. A fertilized embryo "floats" in the uterus for five months as the cells divide and multiply slowly until the mother's hormones trigger fast growth when it will attach to the uterus and develop normally over the next five months. This allows mating to take place when the animals are in peak condition but also for the fawns to be born when the climate is favorable.

BELOW FAMILY PLANNING

A roe deer fawn at just a few days old. The deer mate in early fall, chasing the females and flattening the forest underbrush in the shape of a figure eight (a roe ring). Females give birth the following June, usually to two spotted kids of opposite sexes.

BLENDING IN

A pair of wild boar piglets. Birth (called farrowing) takes place in spring. Generally a litter consists of five piglets but up to thirteen may be born, Initially the piglets have stripes along their backs to help camouflage them in the dappled forest so that they are more difficult for predators to spot. As the pigs grow and become strong enough to attack or avoid predators, these stripes gradually fade away.

MORNING GLORY

A giraffe with her
baby on the African
savanna. Birth usually
occurs early in
the morning with
the young arriving at
the first light of day.
The baby giraffe
scrambles to its feet
within minutes of
birth. It must be able
to outrun predators
as soon as possible.

RAISING A FAMILY

pp. 472–473 STANDING OUT

African elephants are very protective of their young. Usually all members of the herd are related and will act as a protective family force to shield a young one from any potential danger.

OPPOSITE   FURRY BABIES

A Cape hare mother and her baby: Cape hares occur throughout Africa, not just on the Cape. Females usually give birth to twins, which are born with fur and with their eyes already open.

BELOW   SCENTLESS HARES

Very young Cape hare babies do not seem to have a body scent and are ignored by dogs. They are weaned and independent when only a month old.

Young lynxes start eating meat when they are only one month old and are fully weaned at around three months. The cubs stay with their mother for about a year.

BELOW BEAUTIFUL BABIES

Female Canadian lynxes give birth to between one and six cubs — usually two to four — with streaked and spotted fur.

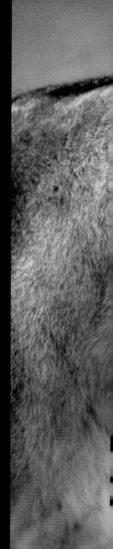

KEEPING CUBS SAFE

A lioness carrying her cub in the Masai Mara, Kenya. Lion cubs are born blind and helpless, weighing only about 3 pounds (1.5 kg). The mother moves her cubs from one hiding place to another to keep them safe, carrying them in her mouth.

pp. 486–487 STAYING SAFE

A mother cheetah with her cub. From birth until about three months, cubs have a grey mantle of hair on their nape, shoulders, and back. This is thought to help camouflage the cubs in the grass, keeping them safe from predators.

OPPOSITE FEED ME!

A wolf cub begs for food. Cubs cannot maintain their body heat until they are three weeks old so their mother stays with them in the den to keep them warm. She is dependent on her mate and other adult wolves in the pack to bring her food. Both parents and older siblings share the duties involved in raising cubs.

BELOW FRESH FOOD

A coyote parent regurgitates food for its pup. The pups are born in a den and suckle for five to seven weeks. Both parents provide the youngsters with regurgitated food but the mother does not allow the father to come all the way into the den. Only about 20 per cent of coyote pups survive their first year.

NOT FUSSY FEEDERS

This hyena is with her young near the safety of the den. An average hyena litter has two to three pups. Spotted hyena pups are born black and change color as they grow. Brown hyena pups are born with their adult coloring. These pups nurse from any willing lactating female.

SPYING DANGER

Grizzly bears are
solitary animals,
except for females
who have cubs. Here
a grizzly bear mother
is on the look out for
danger while out with
her four cubs. Cubs
remain with their
mothers for at least
two-and-a-half years.

Pygmy hippopotamus calves are born on land but common hippos give birth underwater. The female moves away from the main body of the herd as the time for birth approaches.

OPPOSITE   QUICK GROWTH

A Weddell seal mother with her pup in the Weddell Sea, Antarctica. Mother seals provide their pups with a very rich nourishing milk so they grow quickly, from 60 pounds (27 kg) at birth, to about 200 pounds (90 kg) in about seven weeks.

BELOW   DELAYED PREGNANCY

Female seals give birth on land. They mate again immediately but the foetus does not develop. A full year can pass before the female returns to land for the next cycle of birth and conception.

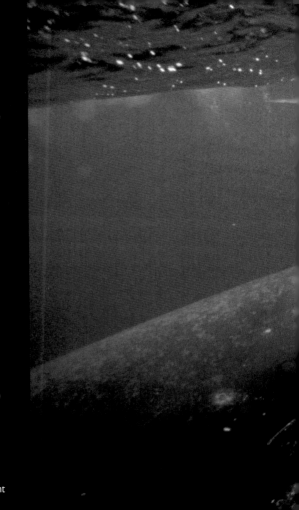

BIG BABIES

Every two to three
years, a female
humpback whale
bears a calf some
10–15 feet (3–4.5 m)
long and weighing in
at about a ton. The
calf soon grows as it
nurses frequently on
her rich milk which
has a 45 to 60 percent
fat content.

It takes about 17 months for a young killer whale to develop inside its mother. Calves are born fully submerged and start to nurse about one hour after birth, suckling from nipples inside the mother's mammary slits.

OPPOSITE SWANS EGGS

Whooper swans breed in boggy areas with pools and reedy lakes. They lay 3 to 7 eggs that take 35 days to incubate in a secluded nest. The young leave the nest quite soon after hatching and are tended by both parents.

BELOW PROLIFIC BREEDERS

The dunnock, or hedge sparrow, lives throughout Europe and Asia. Females lay 3 to 6 pale blue eggs which hatch after about 12 days. They have 2 to 3 clutches each year.

This white-winged black tern is on a floating nest made
by both parents. These birds nest on top of muskrat
houses, floating roots, driftwood, or boards. Often, the
flimsier nests are destroyed by wind and waves. During
the breeding season, the terns catch insects such as
dragonflies, mayflies, moths and beetles in mid-air.

These are white-winged black tern hatchlings in their
nest. Black terns defend a small territory just around
the nest. The downy hatchlings move about on the
nest for about two weeks and start to fly and fish at
only three to four weeks old.

A gannet nesting colony at Cap St. Mary, in
Newfoundland. Gannetries like this are located on steep
cliffs and small offshore islands. The nest is made from
seaweed, sticks, moss, debris, feathers, fish skeletons,
and droppings. Nests are usually set in regular lines,
allowing the birds to cram the maximum number
of nests into a site.

GANNETS ON GUARD
At least one parent is always present to make sure the
young ones do not tumble off the steep cliffside.

RAISING A FAMILY

Sparrow chicks in their nest. The disappearance of nesting sites, increase in predators and competitors, disease, and loss of food sources, have all led to the decline of the urban sparrow.

BELOW   MANY BROODS

Swallow hatchlings in their nest. Swallows and martens build their nests in trees, cliffs, riverbanks, and buildings. They raise two or three broods a year.

RAISING A FAMILY

A blackcap male feeding his young. The blackcap's nest is usually built in low shrub and three to six eggs are laid. The male sometimes builds several rough nests before the female finds one she likes, and even then she may decide to add the finishing touches herself or even to reject the nest and build her own.

OPPOSITE   LONG TERM NESTS

A white stork nesting. A stork's nest is often huge and can measure over 6 feet (2 m) in diameter and be about 10 feet (3 m) deep. The nest may be used for many years and male storks are as attached to their nests as they are to their partners.

BELOW   A PARENT'S JOB IS NEVER DONE

Baby birds are always hungry. Bird parents often spend all their time foraging for food for their young.

adult sea gull is regurgitating food for its young. These opportunists will seize e food such as crabs and small fish, or scavenge whatever is available in order to ep up the supply for their fast-growing brood.

517   TWO-PARENT FAMILY

snowy owl parent passes a mouse to its young. This species nests on the ground. ome five to fourteen eggs are laid, usually every other day over the course of veral days. The pure white chicks are cared for by both parents.

POSITE   SIMPLE NESTS

ttle terns build simple, small scrape nests in the sand. The inconspicuous nests d camouflaged eggs and chicks help them remain hidden from predators.

LOW   QUICK LEARNERS

vocet chicks like these can run about and feed themselves within a few hours om hatching and fledge at around 35 to 42 days.

RAISING A FAMILY

Swans mate for life and form a very close family unit, raising three to five chicks in a large nest made of moss and sedge that is lined with down and can measure about 3 feet (1 m) across. It is usually placed at the water's edge or on a small island.

BELOW   SWANNING AROUND

Baby swans, or cygnets, are raised by their parents. During the breeding season males become very territorial and will attack intruders quite aggressively. The cygnets are covered in fluffy grey down when they hatch but this is gradually replaced by their white adult plumage. The parents protect their offspring quite aggressively for the first few months, but then drive them away before the next breeding season begins when a new brood will be raised.

Emperor penguin pairs with their chicks in the Weddell Sea, Antarctica. The female lays a single egg, which the male incubates, keeping it warm on his feet, covered by his warm brood pouch, for 72 days. The male feeds the newly hatched chick with fluid produced by a gland in his oesophagus, losing half his body weight in the process. When the female returns with food, the male crosses the snow and ice to the sea to catch fish for the family.

OPPOSITE   QUITE A MOUTHFUL

In Sangalakki, Indonesia, a gold specs jawfish male incubates eggs in his mouth. He will be unable to feed until this task is complete.

BELOW   TIME TO GO

Jawfish usually spawn at dusk or dawn and are called "mouthbrooders." Here a ring-eye jawfish male in Borneo, having taken care of the unhatched eggs in his mouth for a week, now expels the young larvae.

pp. 530–531 LEMON SHARKS

A newborn lemon shark pup swims away from its mother in the Caribbean. Litters consist of about 36 young, each about 18 inches (46 cm) long at birth.

OPPOSITE STANDING GUARD

This goby is guarding his eggs laid near Mabul Island, in Borneo. During their courtship ritual, goby males coax the females into their lairs to lay their eggs and then stay on or near this nest for up to three weeks to protect several thousand eggs.

BELOW TRANSSEXUAL FISH

All clownfish are born male. They live in small groups led by the largest male who eventually becomes a female. The second largest male breeds with her. If the female dies, the breeding male will turn into a female and the largest male in the group will take his place as the breeding male.

SEE-THROUGH FROGS

A glass frog parent is guarding a batch of eggs mounded on a leaf in the Belize rainforest. The skin of a glass frog is translucent so its intestines and bones can be seen, hence its name.

Salamanders and newts have an elaborate courtship procedure whereby the sperm is delivered to the female in special capsules which may be transferred via the nose or enter directly through her skin.

BELOW HEATED INCUBATION

A British grass snake guards its eggs. These are usually laid in a warm pile of rotting vegetation, manure, grass cuttings, or compost. Here the warmth and moistness will help their incubation (a temperature of at least 70°F/21° C is needed). Grass snakes mate soon after they emerge from hibernation in April or May. From 8 to 40 leathery skinned eggs are laid in June to July and hatch after about ten weeks.

A young Parson's chameleon in Madagascar sits on its mother's head. The female produces from 16 to 30 eggs once every two years and buries them in moist soil. Their incubation takes longer than a year. At 30 inches (76 cm), this is the largest chameleon in the world.

Many young animals have a lot to learn before they can survive by themselves. Some learning behavior is governed by instinct; for example most baby birds need to learn how to fly. At a certain moment in their growth period the young birds simply launch themselves into the air. This is high risk behavior — mortality among birds

PLAYING &
LEARNING

learning to fly is very high — but the desire to seems to be both inborn and irresistible. Baby mammals also need to learn a lot before setting out on their own, from how to find food to how to avoid becoming someone else's supper. They learn these skills either by themselves through trial and error or they are taught by parents or relatives.

PLAYING & LEARNING

p. 541 FEMALES LEADERS

Young African elephants playing together in Etosha National Park, Namibia. Baby elephants enjoy fun and games and learn about the herd and their environment through play. Female elephants live together in herds led by an older female, called a matriarch. She heads a group that is usually made up of her sisters, daughters, and female cousins, all of whom help one another with the care and education of the young.

HAVING FUN

A young chimpanzee playing with an adult that seems willing to tolerate fairly frisky behavior. Chimpanzees develop highly complex social relationships which were little understood until Jane Goodall's intense groundbreaking research in Tanzania in the 1960s.

pp. 544–545 FISHING FOR TERMITES

Chimpanzees are among the few animals that make and use tools. Here a mother chimpanzee is using a twig to fish termites out of their mound. The baby chimpanzee will learn this skill from its mother.

OPPOSITE RAIN DROPS KEEP FALLING ON MY HEAD

An adult orangutan and a young one having fun catching rain in their open mouths in Gunang Leuser National Park, in Indonesia. A youngster will stay with its mother until it is about eight years old.

BELOW PLAYING GAMES

An olive baboon plays with a tiny baby in the Masai Mara, Kenya. All sorts of behavior will be tolerated from the small baboons while they are still in their dark "baby" fur.

TIME TO LEARN

Young chimpanzees playing in a tree in East Africa. They will have from three to seven years to develop a wide range of social and physical skills (such as climbing, using tools, making sleeping nests, wrestling, and so on) under the care of their mothers before they leave to develop independently. They will be fully grown at twelve to thirteen years old.

Leopard cub playing with its mother in the Masai Mara, Kenya. Leopard litters can contain up to seven young, but most consist of one or two blind, furry cubs. They begin following their mother at about six weeks, learning how to hunt from her.

OPPOSITE   ESTABLISHING A PECKING ORDER

These "not-quite-adult" lions are playing in the Okavango Delta, in Botswana. Play fighting helps to hone hunting skills and will in due course serve to establish their status in the pride.

BELOW   LIVING DANGEROUSLY

This cheetah cub is just a few weeks old. Females give birth to 1 to 5 cubs and they need to learn survival and hunting tactics quickly. Sadly, their death rate is very high and up to 90 percent of young cheetahs are killed during their first few weeks by lions, hyenas, or eagles.

pp. 554–555 SURVEILLANCE TOUR

A female cheetah with two cubs passes in front of a herd of wildebeest in Kenya's Masai Mara. The young ones will stay with their mother until they are about two years old.

PLAYING & LEARNING

OPPOSITE   BOBCAT LIFE SPANS

Bobcat cubs are independent of their mothers at about 10 to 12 months. In the wild, bobcats only live up to 12 years old, with many dying much younger. In captivity they can reach their mid twenties.

BELOW   SEEING THE WORLD

Bobcat cubs nurse until they are about two months old and are then weaned onto a diet of meat. They follow their mother during her nocturnal hunting trips, learning how to hunt and kill for themselves.

A European wildcat mother and her kitten. Wildcats give birth to 2 to 4 young in a den, cave, fox hole, or hollow tree. The kittens are independent after only 4 to 5 months.

OPPOSITE   FIERCE HUNTERS

A Canadian lynx cub playing on a log. Lynxes are now endangered and are protected in some parts of the world. Lynx can take prey up to four times their size so if they enter populated areas may be killed by farmers as well as by traffic on the roads.

BELOW   LITTLE LYNXES

A pair of Canadian lynx cubs. The adults mate in late winter and the females give birth to 2 to 4 cubs in the spring. The youngsters stay with their mother throughout their first winter, learning from her and developing their survival skills.

PLAYING & LEARNING

pp. 562–563 PLAY FIGHTING

These young white Bengal tigers are play fighting in the water, in India. Play fighting with siblings develops coordination and muscles, good preparation for the hunting skills the cubs will need to survive. Tiger mothers begin taking their cubs to kill sites when they are about two months old. She begins teaching them to hunt at about six months; they will be independent of her when they are about 15 months old.

INTELLIGENT PUPPIES

A hyena pup in Africa. Play is an important part of the development of any intelligent animal and hyenas are highly intelligent predators, even more so than lions. Some scientists have suggested that hyenas are almost as smart as the great apes.

PLAYING & LEARNING

These male polar bear siblings are play fighting in Manitoba, Canada. The cubs are born during winter hibernation. It will be 2 to 3 years before they are fully weaned and independent, so there is plenty of time for play and learning how to be a successful bear in an especially harsh environment.

CHILDHOOD HABITS LINGER

These adult giant pandas are enjoying a romp as they eat bamboo in the Qionglai Mountains, in Sichuan, China. Pandas feed almost entirely on bamboo and spend some 12 hours a day munching the stems and leaves. There are only about 1000 giant pandas left in the wild.

PLAYING & LEARNING

Meerkats (also called suricates) are small burrowing mammals that live on the plains of southern Africa. These young ones in the Kalahari are just a few weeks old. They do not come above ground until at least three weeks of age and stay with "babysitters" near the burrow for a week or so before joining the adults on their first foraging party.

OPPOSITE ABSENT FATHERS

A fallow deer fawn. Usually a single fawn is born. For most of the year, fallow deer live in two distinct groups: one of adult females with yearlings and fawns; the other of bucks. The groups join up only when it is time for the rut so the fathers have nothing to do with the care of their young.

ABOVE HIDDEN AWAY

A young female nyala, a South African antelope that lives alone or in small groups in forested areas. The newborn calves are left alone after birth and for their first three weeks lie still in the grass, except when their mothers return to feed them, thus avoiding the notice of predators. Nyala are generally very shy and cautious.

PLAYING & LEARNING

A spotted deer fawn in a grassy meadow. Fawns learn to be shy and cautious and to hide or run from predators that, depending on location, can include people, tigers, leopards, coyotes, foxes, badgers, raccoons, fire ants, and vultures.

OPPOSITE NECKING

These giraffes are "necking" in a play fight in East Africa, practicing an important technique. In adults, necking is initiated by a challenger giraffe who will fight for dominance over females by clubbing opponents with his head and neck. Thus, the stronger, larger-necked male will gain the dominant role in fathering offspring.

BELOW LOOK AND LEAP

A common zebra foal jumps over its resting mother in Kenya, East Africa. A family herd usually consists of mothers and their young plus a head stallion. Young males travel in their own "bachelor" herds until they are able to gather together a herd of their own.

PLAYING & LEARNING

KIT IN THE GRASS

A baby wild rabbit is called a kit, which is short for kitten. Some rabbits can hop along at a surprising speed as they scamper and play but young rabbits seem to "walk," rather than to hop.

ARE YOU COMPLETELY SURE ABOUT THIS, MOM?

A Mexican spotted owl and its fledgling appear to be contemplating flight. Spotted owls mate in February and March and the females lay 1 to 3 eggs in April and May. After about one month's incubation, the chicks hatch. They fledge just over a month later and are completely independent by fall.

As chicks near the end of their infancy they begin to fledge. Adult feathers start to appear, replacing any fluffy down the chick may have had initially. The young birds, like this Eastern screech owl fledgling, teeter precariously on branches or peer anxiously from their nests as they move toward flight.

BELOW THE MASTERY OF FLIGHT

Some young birds flutter to the ground on their inaugural flight, where many are eaten by cats and other predators. If the nest is higher up, unskilled youngsters can have disastrous crashes when they first set out. Like the kestrel fledgling shown here, many young birds spend time on the nest exercising their wings and practicing for flight.

pp. 590–591   MONOGAMOUS GEESE

A mother goose introduces her goslings to the world. Geese normally mate for life and the females lay from 3 to 13 unspotted eggs each year. The young are mobile as soon as they hatch although they stay with their parents for almost a year.

OPPOSITE   KEEPING THEIR FEET ON THE GROUND

Two-week-old nandu (rhea) chicks tiptoe across the grass on their three-toed feet. These South American birds will not be fully mature until two years of age. Strong swimmers and fast runners, they will never learn to fly.

ABOVE   CHECKING THINGS OUT

A one-day-old black-winged stilt chick explores it surroundings, having emerged from its nest on the ground in a loose colony of breeding birds. The chick will grow up to be tall and slender with long legs and a long thin bill.

sting structures or build new

ifferent reasons. The first and

for a home is simply to find

ements (heat, cold, wind, rain,

But a good den, burrow, nest,

an also offer protection from

ed as a storehouse for excess

a nursery for giving birth and

M E S

ng. Some animals, such as

ter builders whose tall mounds

tioning and humidity control.

social weaver bird, build vast

scores of individual nests each

rivate entrance. Beavers cut

use them to dam rivers to raise

re building their sturdy lodges.

imal homes is endless.

A pygmy owl peers out of its nest hole in a tree in Sweden. These tiny owls often live in the hollows of trees and, in the Americas, may occupy hollow acti, sometimes year after year.

OPPOSITE RESTING SPOT

A mother and young Milne Edward's sportive lemur. These creatures make their homes in the dry forests of northern Madagascar.

BELOW SLOWLY DOES IT

A potto in its daytime resting hole in a tree in an Africa rainforest. Once out of its home, the potto moves slowly along the branches. If danger threatens it freezes, staying perfectly still for several hours if necessary.

pp. 600–601   BIRTHING DENS

A female jaguar and her four-day-old cub in its birth den in Amazonia, Brazil. The cubs stay with their mother for several years before leaving to find their own territory. Jaguars live mainly in forests and swamp lands where the females set up homes in dens among rocks, vegetation, or in riverbank holes.

COYOTE HOMES

A coyote pup looks out from the safety of its den. Coyotes don't generally dig their own dens but find and enlarge comfortable spots in rocky crevices, logs, or caves. Sometimes they take over the abandoned dens of other animals.

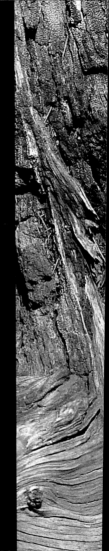

Wolf cubs about to venture out of their lair. Wolves live in homes called lairs that are usually located in a hollow tree or cave, or are dug into the ground by the wolves themselves.

OPPOSITE SCENTLESS SLEEP

A fox in a tree trunk den. The fox is an adaptable creature and may live in a den or burrow that it has dug out for itself or occupy another creature's former home. When a fox settles to sleep in its den, its scent weakens and once it is snugly asleep, it gives off no scent at all.

ABOVE HOME SWEET HOME

A red fox vixen suckles her cubs in the safety of her den.

pp. 608–609 BORROWED HOMES

A river otter emerging from its riverside den.
These playful creatures live in underground dens,
although they rarely build them themselves;
instead they move into abandoned beaver lodges
or homes built by other creatures, such as old
woodchuck dens.

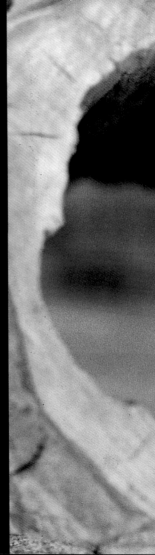

VERSATILE MARTENS

Beech martens are mainly active at night and can
live very close to humans without ever being seen.
They can be found from Spain to Mongolia, mostly
in rocky environments (which is why they are
sometimes called stone martens). They live in
forests and on mountain slopes at altitudes up
to 13,000 feet (4,000 m), in dens in hollow trees,
abandoned burrows, rocky crevices, or, when
near houses, in outbuildings.

is hibernating dormouse is curled up asleep in its nest. Dormice are
cturnal and live mostly in Europe in tree holes, burrows, or under building
ofs or floors. They may hibernate for over six months of the year if the
eather is cool, waking for brief periods to eat food stored nearby.

POSITE FOND OF THE SUN

female garden dormouse peeps out of her nest hole. Dormice like to live
woodland edges and clearings, rough commons, coarse hedges, and
ergrown gardens. They enjoy sunlight so do not choose deep woodland.

LOW MESSING UP LAWNS

his pocket gopher is in an underground tunnel. These ground squirrels
uild extensive burrow systems called lodges where they store food, and
ften, like moles, create mounds of disturbed soil in gardens and lawns.

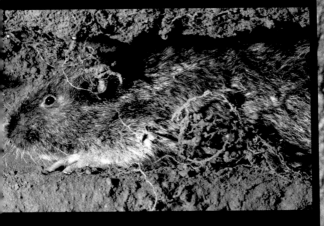

DAM BUILDERS

A beaver carrying out repair work on its dam. Beavers like to construct their lodges in deep water so that the entrances are beneath the surface. If the river or lake where they choose to live is not deep enough, they will build a dam. Both the dome-shaped lodge and the dam are built to last using tree trunks, branches, weeds, stone, and mud.

INSET   NEARLY THERE

Beavers have big, sharp incisor teeth which they use to cut down even quite large trees. They drag the trees to the water and use them in their dams and lodges.

HOMES

These dwarf mongooses are living in an abandoned termite mound in Kenya. The 37 species of mongoose live in a variety of homes, from burrows to hollow trees, to nests in vegetation, and rock crevices.

BELOW   SHARED RANGES

A meerkat surveys the world from its burrow entrance in the Tswalu Kalahari reserve in South Africa. Some 30 or so meerkats will live together in a home range that provides shelter in burrows or rock crevices, complete with feeding sites and nest chambers.

A European mole emerges from its burrow, in the United Kingdom. These small blind creatures are widespread in Europe and Asia and from southern Canada to northern Mexico. They build extensive burrow systems in soft soil or hard sand.

nine-banded armadillo leaving its burrow. Armadillos are normally solitary creatures but some share an extensive burrow system.

pp. 624-625 BIRD CITIES

A nesting colony of weaver birds in Kenya. Many species of weaver birds make huge woven nests from grass and twigs suspended from a tree.

OPPOSITE IMPRESSING THE LADIES

A male African masked weaver bird building a nest. He hopes this nest will attract the interest of a female.

BELOW RECYCLED NESTS

House martins peep out of their mud nest. House martins nest in colonies, building tiers of mud cups under the eaves of houses. If undisturbed, these nests will be used for several years.

A group of three cormorants nesting in a tree. These birds build nests in places that are high enough to be safe from most predators and close to a supply of fish. Their bulky nests are made of sticks, weeds, and seaweed. Trees that are consistently used for nest sites may die from the chemical impact of the copious bird droppings.

LITTLE OWLS

A little owl in an oak tree den. Little owls live in woodlands, fields, and coastal and semi-desert areas. They nest in secret places such as farmland hedges, ruins and old walls, tree and cliff holes, pollarded willows, and rabbit burrows. Their chicks leave the nest after about 26 days.

OPPOSITE   A PRICKLY HOME

The gila woodpecker is a medium-sized woodpecker that builds its nest in holes made in the saguaro cactus or in mesquite trees.

BELOW   ON THE INSIDE LOOKING OUT

A western screech owl in a saguaro cactus cavity in the Sonora Desert in Arizona. This bird inhabits woodlands, forests, and deserts from Alaska to Texas and Mexico. It nests in tree cavities, holes in cliffs, old woodpecker nests, and giant saguaro cacti

NESTING
UNDERGROUND

A bee-eater bird
emerging from its
underground nest.
These birds live in
colonies in open
country in tropical
and sub-tropical
regions of the Old
World. They nest
in short tunnels in
sandy banks and
cliffs or on steep
slopes — such as
river and canal
banks — and in
ravines and
quarries. In South
Africa, these birds
usually dig a new
breeding burrow
each year but
studies in Europe
suggest that there
they re-use nests
made in previous
years.

pp. 636–637
GIANT LIZARDS

A Komodo dragon hatchling emerging from its burrow on Komodo Island. These huge lizards live exclusively on the Indonesian islands of Komodo and its near neighbors.

At night, adult Komodo dragons sleep in caves or among tree roots.

HELPING EACH OTHER

A Clark's anemonefish, hiding in the tentacles of a sea anemone. These fish are immune to the sea anemone's poisonous tentacles. In return for their secure home the fish clean the anemone and keep it safe from some of its own predators.

OPPOSITE   SOCIAL INSECTS

A saxon wasps nest, exposed to show worker wasps busily tending the nest.
These wasps live in southern Britain. They build their large nests out of a kind
of paper that they produce themselves from wood fiber.

BELOW   BEES WITH BAD ATTITUDES

A swarm of killer bees on their nest in Venezuela. These bees arose in the 1950s
when Brazilian scientists attempted to improve honey production of the local bees
by crossing them with an African bee. The resulting hybrid was aggressive and easily
agitated, hence its name: the killer bee.

A SERIES OF HOMES

This bright orange hermit crab lives in a triton shell in the waters of the Great Barrier Reef, off Australia. Usually the entire body of a crab is covered with a hard, calcified protective "armor." The hermit crab, however, has a soft, vulnerable abdomen and so it uses abandoned shells for protection, especially old whelk shells. As the hermit crab grows, it has to "move house" by finding a larger shell.

cheetah in hot pursuit of an antelope, a pack of
wolves closing in on a deer, a spider lying in wait
for a fly, or a monkey cramming its mouth full of
berries: these are all key moments in a never-
ending drama that is played out every day in the
animal world — the search for food. Irrespective
of whether they eat plants or animals, or a

FINDING
FOOD

combination of the two, almost all living creatures
need to find food on a regular basis. Some
animals, including tigers and lions, are active
hunters. They spend time and energy hunting
down live prey. Others, such as hyenas and sea
gulls, combine hunting with scavenging, while
others, like manatees and horses, are herbivores.

OKE THE STEM IN THE HOLE ...

his young female chimpanzee in the Gombe National Park in
anzania is called Golden. She has learned from her mother how
o use a stem as a tool to remove termites from a termite mound.

p. 647   NOT FUSSY EATERS

A sea gull with prey in beak. Sea gulls are not fussy eaters and will scavenge for food as
well as skimming fish from the surface waters of the sea. They will pick through waste
and sewage, steal eggs, prey on young birds and mammals, and fly inland to find worms

Here Golden practices removing termites from a termite mound with a stem and successfully negotiates the insects into her mouth.

OPPOSITE BAMBOO DIET

A grey bamboo lemur in the rainforest of Madagascar. A critically endangered lemur, up to 98 percent of its diet is comprised of bamboo. It tears apart mature wooden bamboo poles with its powerful jaws to reach the soft pith inside, as well as eating new bamboo shoots and young leaves. Some (but not all) also eat mature leaves.

BELOW A VEGETARIAN DIET

A ring-tailed lemur eating cactus in Berenty Reserve, Madagascar. These creatures eat fruit, bark, leaves, grass, and tree resin which they chisel out with their sharp incisors.

pp. 652–653 CRAB-EATERS

Longtailed macaques are also known as crab-eating macaques. This one on the coast of Sumatra, in Indonesia, has just caught a crab which is still dangling from its paw. Longtailed macaques catch the crabs in mangrove swamps and sometimes get pinched in the process.

DRUNKEN RAIDERS

Raccoons eat fish, insects, small mammals, fruit, berries, corn, eggs, and birds. Raccoons are very intelligent animals and are rumored to wash their food before eating. Not everyone agrees with this theory. Raccoons are also famous as garbage raiders and have even been known to uncork wine bottles, drink the contents, and get thoroughly drunk!

A cheetah with its catch. Cheetahs eat gazelle, antelopes, hares, and many kinds of birds, including young ostriches. They stalk their "menu-choice" and then make a sudden swift dash, at speeds of up to nearly 70 miles (112 km) per hour. They knock their prey down and then deliver the fatal bite to the throat. Sometimes cheetahs work together to capture larger victims, such as zebra.

pp. 658–659 A VARIED MENU
Hyenas with kill. These scavengers live on carrion, such as the remains of kills by lions, but also eat small mammals, birds, lizards, snakes, insects, and fruit. Hyenas living near the coast enjoy an even more varied diet, adding mussels, dead fish, and stranded seal or whale corpses to their varied menu.

OPPOSITE   SUPREME HUNTERS

Like all cats, lynxes are superb hunters.
Everything about their bodies and
behavior is suited to the hunt. Here a lynx
catches a rabbit in the winter snow.

BELOW   GOOD TEETH FOR THE JOB

Lynxes are solitary, nocturnal hunters that
prey on fawns, rodents, hares, goats, sheep,
and ground-based birds such as grouse.
They have sharp canine teeth to hold and
kill prey and strong cutting teeth to chew
food into digestible pieces.

pp. 662–663   ALL-ROUND HUNTERS

Mountain lions prey on a wide range of animals, from chipmunks, squirrels, and porcupines to deer, moose, and buffalo. They also kill and eat domestic livestock if given the chance. A normal adult mountain lion eats about 10 pounds (5 kg) of meat every day. Mountain lions that live above the timberline hunt by day; those at lower altitudes are generally nocturnal.

DOMESTIC PREY

This wolf in the Italian Apennines has caught a sheep. Wolves often hunt together in packs and will — depending on their habitat — take deer, caribou, moose, and wild horses, as well as smaller fry, including crabs, rabbits, fish, and mice.

A male red deer in its winter coat. These deer feed on grass, heather, leaves, and buds, usually eating in the early morning or late afternoon to evening.

BELOW   BENEATH THE WINTER SNOW

A reindeer in the snow. In the summer, reindeer crop the grass and other plants in the tundra. In winter, however, they have to work harder to find sustenance, scraping away the snow with their hooves to find the lichen and hardy plants below.

pp. 670–671   HAPPY HOUR

A nyala drinking. These antelopes browse on young grasses, leaves, shoots, bark, and fruit, sometimes standing up on their hind legs to reach foliage.

OPPOSITE   WHATEVER'S ON THE MENU

Hares and rabbits eat a wide variety of grasses as well as clover, dandelions, buds, berries, roots, fungi, and ferns. In winter, they nibble twigs, shrub and tree bark, and bush stems.

BELOW   A WESTERN DIET

Prairie dogs graze on the rolling plains of the western United States, from Montana to Mexico. With their sharp teeth, they munch away on roots, leaves, and flowers.

OPPOSITE A TANTALIZING CHERRY

A Siberian chipmunk reaches up to nibble a cherry on a tree in Japan. These tiny creatures eat fruit, vegetables, grasses, and aquatic plants.

BELOW SAP SIPPERS

A British grey squirrel reaching down to drink. An adult squirrel will consume nearly 3 ounces (80 g) of shelled nuts each day, as well as eggs, young birds, and insects. Sometimes it will strip the bark from a young tree to sip the sap beneath.

FINDING FOOD

pp. 676–677 HEARTY APPETITES

Elephants eat grass, branches, leaves, bark, and fruit, and supplement their diet with salt whenever they can find it. An adult eats some 350 pounds (160 kg) of vegetation each day.

OPPOSITE   A SEAFOOD DIET

A giant otter eating a fish in Guyana. These otters catch perch and catfish, as well as small caiman, crustaceans, and snakes. They consume up to 9 pounds (4 kg) of seafood each day.

BELOW   FLOATING SEAFOOD PLATTER

A sea otter eating clams near the coast of California. Sea otters enjoy a good seafood platter that includes mussels, chitons, snails, prawns, crabs, abalone, sea urchins, squid, sea star legs and fish, as well as clams which they crush with rocks to open. They often float on their backs with their choice of fare spread out on their stomachs.

OPPOSITE   A NUTRITIOUS MEAL

Ostrich eggs are a great treat for many animals. Here, a lioness raids a full nest of eggs. Not much will be left by the time she has finished.

BELOW   HOW TO BREAK AN EGG — IN ONE EASY LESSON

For smaller animals and birds the ostrich egg's thick shell can be tough to break. This does not deter all of them though. Here, a vulture raises a stone in its beak that it will either drop on the egg or beat against the shell.

pp. 682–683   AN UNDERWATER SNACK

This West Indian manatee is munching on a water hyacinth. Manatees also enjoy other types of grass, mangrove leaves, algae, and water hydrilla.

OPPOSITE   FRUITIVORES

A Jamaican fruit-eating bat in Panama. These bats mainly eat fruit, such as figs, bananas, mangoes, and papaya, but they also eat some pollen, nectar, and insects.

BELOW   NIGHT HUNTERS

A fringe-lipped bat catching a lizard in Panama. These bats hunt at night but, unlike most bats, do not use echo-location to find their prey.

When feeding, spoonbills swish their beaks from side to
side to create currents that bring fish up into their range,
and then promptly snap then up. They also eat frogs,
shrimps, and other crustaceans and aquatic insects.
Both the common and royal spoonbills sport crests
in the breeding season.

ABOVE   REDSHANK DIET

Redshanks (or spotted redshanks) eat insects, mollusks,
crustaceans, and sometimes small fishes and tadpoles. During
the breeding season they also hunt insects, spiders, and worms

Greenshanks feed on small fish but will also indulge in prawns, mollusks, and insects. During the breeding season they feed mainly on insects, especially beetles and their larvae. They stalk their prey, wading through the water pecking or probing with their beaks, and then dashing through the shallows if they spot a small fish within reach. As with most waders, redshanks feed on a variety of small invertebrates that they find in damp fields, meadows, marshes, estuaries, and moorlands.

A flurry of sea gulls diving on fish. These birds are opportunists and will flock to fishing boats for a fast meal when the catch is being gutted. But the tables can be turned on them... a clever young whale in captivity was observed spitting regurgitated fish onto the surface of the water and then surging up to grab the gulls when they came to eat.

EGG THIEF

This crow is stealing an egg from a cormorant's nest. The omnivorous diet of these birds includes eggs and nestlings, plus other small animals, vegetable matter, carrion, and garbage.

OPPOSITE   WARBLER IN WAITING

A garden warbler. All warblers are small, colorful, and extremely active insectivores. They feed on ants and aphids as well as spiders, fruit, and berries. Many forage for their food in the top branches of trees and sometimes wait there to catch insects in flight.

BELOW   ACORNS FOR THE WINTER

Jays are related to crows. These colorful, noisy, perching birds feed mainly on insects, nuts, and seeds, and sometimes on eggs or nestlings. The Eurasian jay collects and stores acorns as a winter treat.

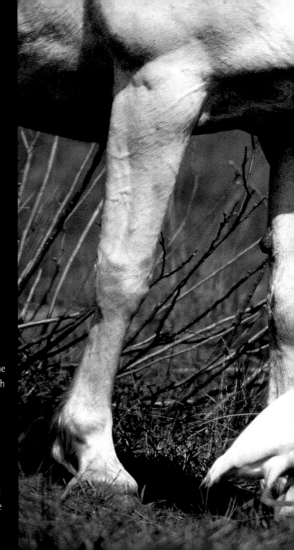

CLEANING SERVICES

Cattle egrets, like the one shown here with a wild Carmargue horse, often live alongside large grazers, such as horses, buffalo, or cattle. They survive by picking ticks and other insects off the larger animal.

pp. 700–701 ANYTHING GOES

A red kite with prey in its beak. This elegant bird of prey is an omnivore and will scavenge and eat carrion, as well as taking small live prey and robbing other birds.

QUITE A BEAKFUL

Puffins are small seabirds that dive to catch their meals and mostly eat small fish, sand eels (as shown here), herring, hake, and crustaceans. Young puffins are fed fish by their parents who can carry several back to the nest at a time — usually about ten fish per trip, but there are reports of over sixty fish being transported in one go.

OPPOSITE   GOOD HEARING

The hawk owl, with its falcon-like wings and a long tail, hunts voles and small birds like thrushes. This one is eating a small rodent in the Canadian Arctic. The hawk owl has good hearing and can locate and capture rodents hidden beneath the snow.

BELOW   A GOOD CATCH

The marsh harrier is a bird of prey that breeds in Europe and Asia and usually winters in Africa. It preys on small mammals, lizards, fish, frogs, insects, and other birds.

CLEANER FISH

These cleaner wrasse are tidying up a rosy goatfish in the Red Sea. Fish gather at wrasse "cleaning stations," often at a fixed time of day, and await their turn for the wrasse to swim into their mouths and feed on decaying food stuck between their teeth. The wrasse also remove diseased tissue and parasites from the outside of the fish. Some wrasse will make special visits to fish whose territorial rights or nervous dispositions prevent them from queuing up with the masses. Both animals benefit from this arrangement: the fish get rid of their parasites and unwanted food and debris and the cleaner wrasse get a good meal.

OPPOSITE   CRUISER RAYS

A spotted eagle ray searches for food buried in the sand in the Red Sea. This is by far the largest eagle ray; it cruises along reef faces and sand flats, scooping its flattened snout through the sand to find tasty morsels such as snails, mussels, and crustaceans, and then crushing the shells with its very hard teeth. These strong swimmers can jump several feet above the surface.

BELOW   ROWS OF TEETH

This coral grouper in the Andaman Sea, near Thailand, swims along with its mouth wide open. Inside, rows of razor-sharp teeth are visible. Coral groupers are active predators that live in a variety of reef habitats. Many feed by lunging at small fish that come too close, especially at sunrise and sunset.

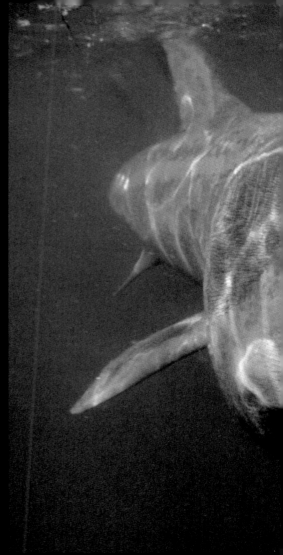

FINDING FOOD

pp. 710–711 GRAZERS

A bullethead parrotfish grazes on coral in the Red Sea, Egypt. It uses its beak to rasp algae, polyps, and other small plant and animal life from the surface of coral and rock. It also eats seaweed and mollusks. The grinding teeth in its throat help to break up food ready for digestion.

BIGMOUTH SHARK

The basking shark, also known as a bigmouth shark, glides along with its mouth wide open. It is a filter feeder and its gill rakers filter out everything that enters it mouth except plankton, fish eggs, and baby fish. Digestion is rapid and the food soon becomes a soupy reddish mass.

pp. 714–715 SURGEONFISH

A green turtle being cleaned by surgeonfish (named for the razor sharp spines at the base of their bodies that can cut like a knife).

OPPOSITE A FULL TIME JOB

A giant tortoise feeding on Santa Cruz Island in the Galapagos. These giants spend most of their waking hours grazing and browsing.

BELOW A VARIED DIET

This hood (or saddleback) tortoise lives on Hood Island in the Galapagos. The Galapagos giant tortoise eats a wide variety of vegetation, including grass and vines, cactus fruit, and both the fallen fruits and spiny pads of the prickly pear.

OPEN WIDE

A brown water snake stretches its jaws wide to swallow a catfish in the Everglades National Park, in Florida. Water snakes hunt by day at the water's edge for fish, frogs, worms, leeches, crayfish, young turtles, salamanders, and small birds and mammals. At night, they catch small fish in shallow water, such as minnows.

pp. 720–721

PREDATORY LIZARD

A darkling beetle serves as a tasty meal for a collared lizard in Colorado. This predatory lizard often hunts in an upright position, running on its hind legs. It preys on grasshoppers, beetles, spiders, and small snakes and lizards.

Whenever an animal is born, the game of life begins anew. Every young creature must learn to escape predators, find food, and reproduce. Animals have many different ways of avoiding attack, including speed, camouflage, threatening postures, well-developed sight, smell, and hearing, the defensive use of poison, armor, horns, teeth, and spines, posting guards, playing

SURVIVAL

dead, or simply hiding away. The environment itself can also be hostile and special skills or attributes are required, for example, to survive extremes of cold and heat, lack or short supply of food and water, or the arrival of new predators or competitors for resources in a given habitat. Sadly, the greatest threat of all to animals is posed by mankind's inability or unwillingness to share our planet's resources.

pp. 722–723 A DANGEROUS HORN

A rhinoceros horn is made of keratin, the same material as fingernails and hair. It is a useful defensive weapon for the animal but some people believe it has aphrodisiac and medicinal powers. This has led to over-hunting, threatening the survival of the rhinoceros.

OPPOSITE NO PLACE TO CALL HOME

The aye aye is another endangered species. As the forests of Madagascar are cleared for growing sugar cane and coconut, the aye-aye loses its habitat.

BELOW A SHRINKING HABITAT

Tarsiers are tiny, nocturnal, forest-dwelling primates; at one time found in Asia, Europe, and North America, they now survive on just a few islands in Southeast Asia.

ABOVE **THE MEANEST AND THE BEST**

Male chacma baboons, like this one in Botswana, engage in aggressive threat displays to establish who ranks highest in their group's social hierarchy.

OPPOSITE **OPEN WIDE**

A crested macaque gives a fine yawn display in the Sulawesi, Indonesia. The males' huge yawns reveal an impressive array of canines in order to assert dominance and avoid conflict.

p. 728 TOUGH LIVES

A Kirk's colobus monkey feeding in a reserve in Zanzibar. Rapid population growth has restricted these monkeys to a small part of the island. Many are hit by cars as the lack of trees forces them down to the ground where they are also more vulnerable to natural enemies such as chimpanzees.

p. 729 ADAPT AND SURVIVE

A Japanese macaque in Japan. Macaques are the most widespread primate, ranging from northern Africa to Japan. These creatures are highly adaptable and this serves them well in the survival stakes.

TREE HOMES

Tree kangaroos are adapted for life in the trees. These strange creatures live in Australia and New Guinea. They appear to have evolved from animals similar to modern kangaroos since they retain features, such as powerful hind legs, that make them suitable for life on the ground. But they have also evolved features to suit their new arboreal homes, such as long tails which they use for balance.

AVOIDING DANGER

Armadillos, like the three-banded armadillo shown here, have excellent defenses to ensure their survival in their Central and South American homes. They often hide in burrows when they sense a danger, but if they meet an enemy head on, will curl up in their bony "coats of armor" until the predator is gone.

NO SNEAKING UP ON THIS BABY

This Demidoff's bushbaby lives in the rainforests of the Democratic Republic of Congo. This nocturnal animal has large eyes and ears that help it to both see and hear in the dark. Although its eyes are fixed in their sockets, a bushbaby can rotate its head nearly 180 degrees in order to see what is going on all around.

A hedgehog crossing the road and a porcupine displaying its quills. Both hedgehogs and porcupines rely on a barrier of fearsome spines to discourage attack by predators. When threatened, they curl up into a ball inside this protective shield. Unfortunately, in areas now criss-crossed with roads, this is not a good way for them to defend themselves against an oncoming car or truck and many are killed on the roads.

A deer's antlers may look like formidable weapons but they are generally used for fighting within the herd during the rut and as proof of masculinity rather than for defense against outsiders. Deer survive mainly by being elusive and shy, keeping a low profile and being fleet of hoof when needs be.

BELOW KEEPING COOL
The summer heat brings another set of problems. This deer is sitting in a pond in an attempt both to cool off and discourage irritating flies.

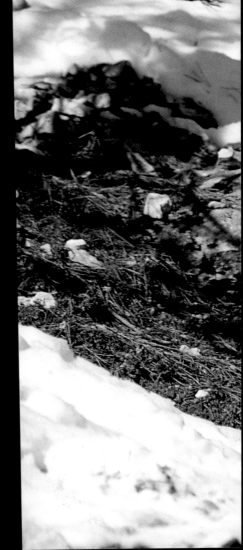

WINTER WOOLIES

An Abruzzi chamois kid in its shaggy winter coat in the Abruzzi national Park, in central Italy. These unique animals, which once ranged over much of the Italian Apennines, are now critically endangered and less than 1000 individuals are believed to be living in the wild.

SHAGGY WINTER COATS

American bison have
thick shaggy coats to
help them survive
the icy winters.
They can also move
quickly and may
stampede when
threatened. Free-
roaming herds
migrate hundreds of
miles and, when they
need to, can run at
about 40 miles
(65 km) per hour.

DANGER IN THE BUSH

The Cape buffalo is
regarded as one of
the most dangerous
and unpredictable
animals in Africa.
Often a herd of these
buffalo will work
together to "mob"
a predator such
as a lion.

Contrary to popular belief, porcupines are not able to throw their quills. But they do swish their quilled tails at attackers and if the victim comes into contact with a quill then it may be driven into the predator's skin. The quills are barbed and therefore difficult and painful to extract. This crested porcupine is scavenging on the ground in central Kenya. Its back quills can be raised into a crest.

OPPOSITE MARCH HARES

Hares are almost invisible during courtship in the long spring grass. Like rabbits, hares breed prolifically with some species producing 2 to 4 litters throughout the year.

ABOVE CAMOUFLAGE

Hares can blend in perfectly with their surroundings making them difficult for predators to see.

The giant elephant shrew is named for its long, almost trunk-like nose although it is unrelated to both the elephant and the shrew. Its long legs help it to escape predators and it uses its "trunk" to find beetles, ants, spiders, worms, and termites in the leaf litter.

OPPOSITE AND BELOW   KEEPING WATCH

Meerkats survive by keeping a constant guard over their burrows and terrain for any sign of danger, such as eagles and jackals. They use a range of alarm calls to indicate different predators. At least one meerkat always stands guard while the others forage or nap. The animal's long tail acts as a tripod to help balance it in its alert upright position.

Warthogs fight "head to head" in Kenya. These animals have large curving tusks with shorter ones below that they use as slashing tools in combat. Prolific breeders, they have a high mortality rate, falling prey to lions, leopards, and jackals, and drowning in the wet season.

ABOVE HELPFUL FATHERS

The free-ranging fox lives in many parts of the northern hemisphere. The male fox helps the family survive by hunting to feed the vixen and cubs and stays around until the young are independent, at about five months old.

BELOW A CHANGE OF COAT

The Arctic fox survives the fierce winter by eating a wide variety
of prey, including hares, but especially lemmings; it will store away
dead lemmings in the snow, ready for eating later. Completely
white in winter when snow covers its surroundings, it becomes
patchy white and brown in spring.

BIG EARS

The smallest member of the dog family, the fennec fox lives in sandy desert areas across North Africa and the Middle East. It eats whatever the desert offers, including rodents, insects, lizards, and dates. It gains most of the liquid it needs to survive from the body fluids of its victims. The fennec fox is distinguished by its large ears. These act as radiators, allowing it to regulate its body temperature in the extreme desert climate.

TOP CATS

Trees help leopards to survive. The broken light of the forest helps them to hide, along with the camouflage of their spotted coats, as they rest in the security of trees. They hunt at night and usually stalk their prey but may observe them from the vantage point of a tree and then leap down from above. The leopard often takes its prey up into a tree to eat and store for later use.

The lynx is a stealthy hunter with strong legs and keen eyesight that allow it to hunt in the twilight. However, these assets do not help it to survive in areas where people live and it is in danger of dying out in many areas.

BELOW WHAT MAKES A CAT WILD?

A female wildcat in the snow. There is very little difference between a wildcat and a domestic tabby. When domestic cats leave human care and become wild they freely interbreed with the local wildcats.

A pair of young lions almost hidden by the long savanna grass. Living in a pride offers extra protection to youngsters and female lionesses take care of — and sometimes even suckle — the young of other members of their group. Lions once ranged right across Africa to India, but now survive only south of the Sahara and in the isolated Gir Forest in India.

OPPOSITE AND BELOW   HOMELESS CATS

At one time mountain lions roamed over all the Americas, from British Columbia to southern Chile and Argentina. Over-hunting and suburban sprawl has pushed them back to just a few isolated areas in the west.

OPPOSITE   A PERFECT DISGUISE

A common potoo (or wood nightjar) disguised as a
branch on a day roost in northeast Brazil. It can stay
perfectly still in this position, bolt upright and
completely invisible, for hours.

BELOW   HOME COLORS

A rock partridge whose feathers blend in perfectly
with the rocks among which it lives.

BACK OFF, BUDDY

A yellow-legged gull attacks a hare which is valiantly trying to defend itself. Usually hares will defend themselves by running away but if cornered will try more active means of defense.

TURNCOATS

Ptarmigans live in the arctic and subarctic areas of America and Eurasia, including Greenland. Like many other creatures in those areas, they have developed a way of changing the color of their coats to suit the season. Here, it is summer and they are a speckled brown color. But. . .

FALL AND WINTER

...when fall comes and snow begins to cover the landscape the ptarmigans start
to molt from brown to white. By winter time, they are completely white.
Their thick coats of white feathers not only help keep them warm but
also make them invisible to predators against the surrounding snow.

OPPOSITE   EYES IN THE BACK OF ITS BUTT

This close-up view of the rear end of an eyespot or false-eyed frog
shows the defensive eye-like markings that suggest the face of a
much larger creature — and so serve to frighten away predators.

BELOW   LEAFY LOOK-A-LIKE

The smokey jungle frog in the rainforest leaf litter of Guyana,
South America, is scarcely recognizable as a tasty meal, since
its brown, leaf-shaped markings help it to disappear into
the background.

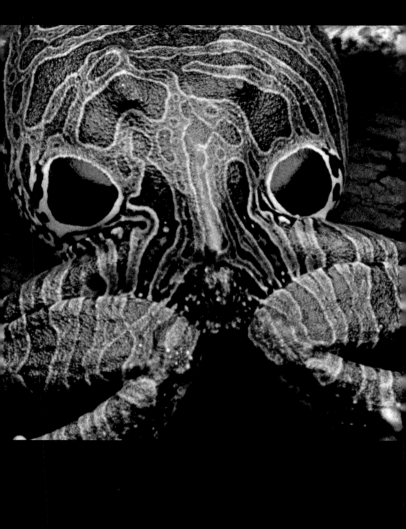

pp. 790–791

ALL PUFFED UP

A common toad is raised up on its front legs and has also swelled up to look much larger — both useful deterrents when confronted by a grass snake with mean intentions.

QUITE A BITE

A striped forest pit viper snake with its young opens its fangs wide to scare off intruders in the Amazon rainforest, Ecuador. The fangs will be folded back inside against the roof of its mouth when they have served their purpose.

ABOVE NOT AN ENEMY IN SIGHT

Young alligators are vulnerable and some are looked after by their mothers for up to three years to give them a better chance of survival. There are not too many threats to an adult alligator, apart from human hunters seeking to turn their tough hides into handbags and shoes. The crocodile family has survived for some 65 million years.

pp. 798–799
NILE LOUNGER

Like most crocodiles, the Nile crocodile has eyes and nostrils on the top of its head so that it can stay in the water, more or less submerged, and approach its prey unnoticed. This one is lounging on the banks of the Nile.

STRONG SHARP SPIKES

The thorny devil lives in the deserts of Australia. It has an armory of spikes covering its entire body to protect it from attack as it forages about on the ground for ants.

OPPOSITE BLENDING IN

A common green iguana is perfectly camouflaged among palm leaves in Cerrado, Brazil. If any birds or mammals do spot and chase it, the iguana may survive by simply dropping from the branches to plummet into the river below.

BELOW GREEN ON GREEN

This female European chameleon is well disguised, green on green, in a bush in Spain. Her narrow leaf-like shape also helps her to hide.

OPPOSITE PLAYING DEAD

When threatened, the grass snake will often fake death to avoid attack. Belly up, with its head thrown back and a sagging jaw, the grass snake does a very good job of seeming dead.

BELOW STAY AWAY FROM ME

The vividly colored nudibranch, or sea slug, uses it glamorous hues to advertise the fact that it is highly poisonous. Its vulnerable soft body contains powerful poisons that predators easily learn to avoid.

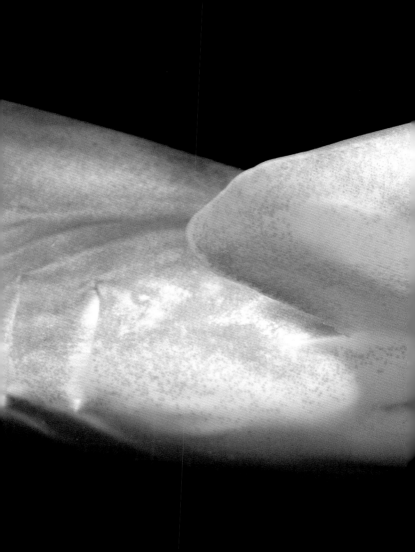

pp. 806–807
STICKING TOGETHER

Hammerhead sharks
may gather into
shoals to gain
protection from
greater numbers.
The young ones
often migrate in
large groups.

pp. 808–809
PATIENT PREDATOR

The Mozambique
scorpionfish hides
patiently in weed-
covered rocks while
it watches out for
prey. It has a nasty
sting if disturbed.

KEEP CLEAR

Lionfish have a
potent poison in
their spines. This can
be fatal to human
beings and will
certainly kill any fish
that comes too close.
The fish's distinctive
appearance warn
intruders to
keep clear.

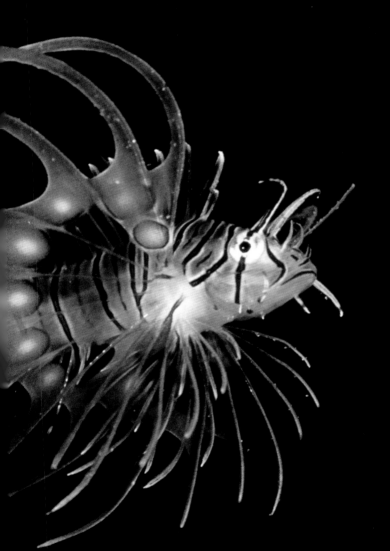

OPPOSITE   GOING FISHING

This female deep sea anglerfish has a lure projecting from her head to attract prey which she will grab with her huge toothy jaws.

BELOW   LETHAL LURKER

A piranha lurks under aquatic plants in Amazonia, Ecuador. With their powerful jaws and razor-sharp teeth, a shoal of piranha can quickly despatch a victim but they do also eat seeds and fruit.

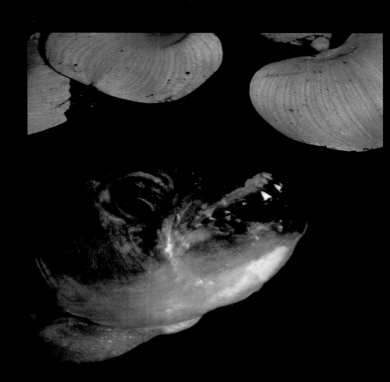

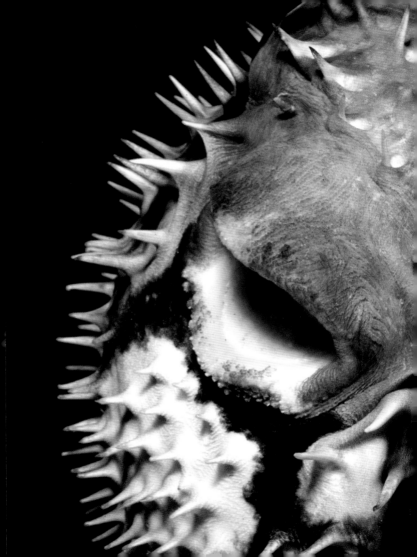

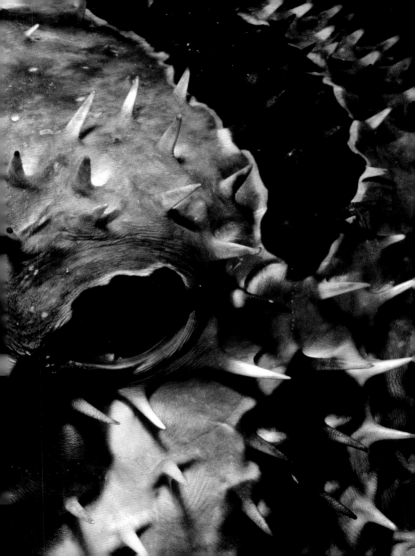

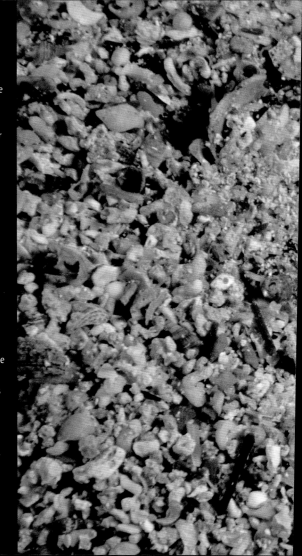

SURVIVAL

STAY AWAY

A black-blotched porcupinefish has "inflated" to become round and spiky (rather like a pincushion) in order to frighten off any predators that invade its space in the Red Sea, near Egypt.

STARGAZER

This stargazer fish is hidden in sand in the Mediterranean Sea off Italy, with just its eyes and mouth exposed, hoping to catch other fish or crustaceans. Organs behind its eyes can produce electric charges so it is well equipped to deal with any threat.

OPPOSITE AND BELOW   A TIGHT FIT

Two veined octopuses seek
refuge inside shells. Octopuses
can also shoot out clouds of ink
to hide behind or they change
color to match their surroundings.
As well as hiding to survive, they
also hide to catch prey, pouncing
and grasping their victims with
their long suckered arms.

SURVIVAL

OPPOSITE AND BELOW   SEAHORSES BLEND IN

Two very different camouflage color schemes are exhibited here. One pygmy
seahorse is hiding in fan coral in the Indo-Pacific . . . while at north Sulawesi on
the Lembeh Strait, Indonesia, another pygmy seahorse has a different range of
spots and dots that perfectly match its coral surroundings.

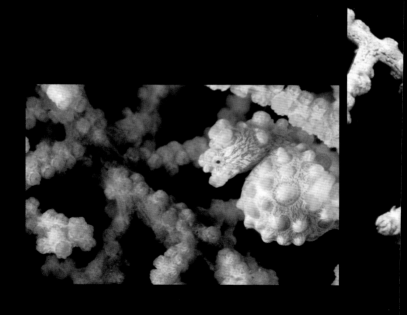

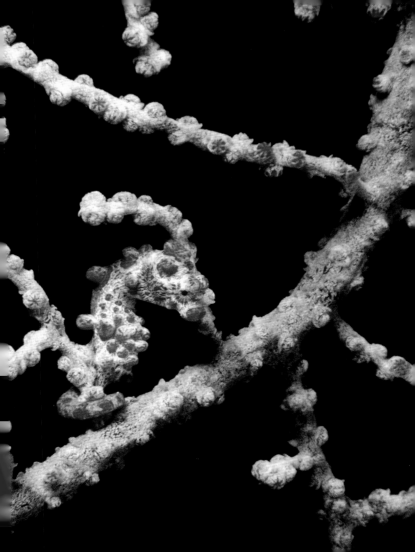

Many animals live together in groups. Often the group takes the form of a harem, with a dominant male commanding a number of females and their offspring. Other groups, such as herds of elephants, are led by a dominant female. The so-called "social insects," such as bees, wasps, ants, and termites, lived together in

ONE OR MANY

large, highly organized associations in which every each member has clearly defined duties and benefits. Whatever the structure of the group, the animals usually stay together in order to improve each individual's chances of survival. Many other animals live entirely alone, only meeting up with others of their species during courtship and mating. For these creatures it is the solitary lifestyle that best guarantees their chances of survival.

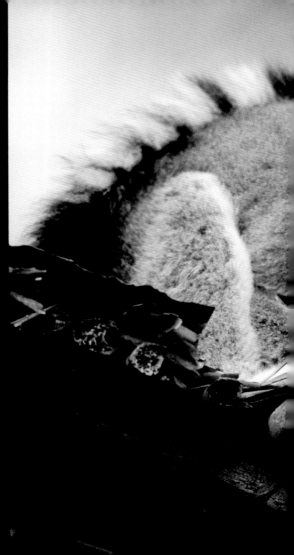

pp. 827 HERDS

Reindeer and caribou live in vast herds, like this one in the Kobuk Valley National Park in Alaska, where the Western Arctic herd numbers some 400,000 individuals. Caribou (known as reindeer in Europe), make long, twice-yearly migrations from the late-spring and summer calving grounds in the far north, to more protected areas in the taiga to the south in winter.

TROOPS

Ring-tail lemurs live together in groups called troops. A troop can contain 5 to 30 lemurs but usually has 15 to 20 individuals, with one dominant female ruling the roost.

ONE OR MANY

Chimpanzees are mankind's closest relatives. They live together in communities of 15 to 150 individuals. The males within a community sometimes form hunting parties and travel widely looking for small mammals, including antelope and other monkeys, to prey on. In this photograph, an alpha male is eating a bushbuck fawn that they have just caught. The other males are begging to be allowed to share some of the kill.

ONE OR MANY

OPPOSITE THE RAREST CAT

Snow leopards live on the "roof of the world" (the high mountains of central Asia). These rare, shy, and solitary creatures only get together during the mating season that runs from January to March. At that time they make long wailing calls that have been mistaken for the dying bellows of the legendary yeti, or abominable snowman.

BELOW KING CHEETAH

By cat standards, a cheetah is relatively social. A mother cares for her offspring for about a year but then siblings will often stay together for many more months. This is a king cheetah whose beautiful markings distinguish it from the normal spotted cheetah.

FEMALE WANDERLUST

A family of cheetahs survey the African plains. Adult female cheetahs usually live alone unless they have cubs with them. The males either live alone or in small groups of two or three individuals. Female cheetahs often have huge territories of up to 300 square miles (800 sq km) since they tend to follow the annual migratory routes of the antelopes they prey on. Many cheetah cubs fall prey to lions and cheetah numbers are generally kept in check by other large carnivores.

pp. 836–837 LONESOME LYNXES

Lynxes usually live alone, although sometimes
they will form small groups.

ABOVE LONG TERM MOMS

Male polar bears are solitary whereas females
are often in the company of from one to four
cubs who live with them for up to three years.
When the female is ready to breed again, an
adult male will begin to follow her and will
chase away the cubs, or she may do this herself.

BROWN BEAR LONERS

The brown bear is generally a loner, except for
females accompanied by cubs. A male may
partner a female for up to two weeks in the
mating season. Other than that, the bears
sometimes meet up at good food sources,
such as garbage dumps or camp sites.

Young red panda cubs seem to stay with the mother for about a year, or until the next litter is about to be born. Other than this — and when they mate — adult red pandas are solitary.

BELOW FOXY FAMILIES

Grey foxes are usually monogamous. Male and female foxes care for their offspring together until fall when the young are about three to four months old. By that time the cubs can hunt for themselves and the family group disperses.

pp. 842–843 SOLITARY HUNTERS

What's on the menu? A lone fox surveys the potential for its next meal, surrounded by ducks. Unlike wolves, these solitary hunters go it alone. They eat a wide variety of foods, including ducks, hens, rabbits, fruits, grasses, caterpillars, and crayfish.

In all the best folk and fairy tales, the red fox is a wily creature, renowned for its cunning. Red foxes are mostly nocturnal but will sometimes venture out in the day. Except for when raising young, the red fox is solitary.

BELOW DHOLEFUL PACKS

The dhole, or Asian wild dog, lives in India, China, and Southeast Asia. These dogs live in packs of 5 to 20 animals. Life in the pack is communal, with adults all helping to feed new mothers and their pups, as well as banding together on hunting trips and to protect members of the group against attack by leopards and tigers.

Unlike foxes, wolves are highly social. They live in extended family packs. Virtually all pack members contribute to the raising of pups and seem to revel in playing with and caring for them. Pack size depends upon the habitat and availability of food.

OPPOSITE PACK BEHAVIOR

Pack members co-operate to maintain territories, find food, and rear their young. They communicate by howling and scent-marking.

BELOW LONE WOLVES

Sometimes a wolf will be driven out of the pack. These lone wolves lead a dangerous life and often follow other wolves, hoping for a chance to become part of a pack again.

MOUNTAIN GOATS

The chamois is a goat antelope that lives in the European alps and other mountainous areas in Europe. The females usually live in flocks. Male kids stay with their mother's flock until they are two to three years old, then they live alone until they are fully mature at about eight years of age. The flocks often disperse during the winter when the animals move down into warmer woodlands.

INTO THE SETTING SUN

A herd of impala browse against the setting sun, in Africa. The females form groups of 30 to 120 individuals. There are also bachelor herds of males (aged over one year) that live separately. Males often leave the bachelor groups to set up a territory close to a female herd in the hope of winning a harem of their own.

SAFETY IN NUMBERS

Deer live together in herds. There are many advantages to living with a large number of your kind

ONE OR MANY

Zebras live on the African savanna, in male dominated harems and bachelor groups of younger males. Sometimes these groups join together to form large herds. Like horses, zebras can often be seen doing mutual grooming which not only helps keep their coats in order but also reinforces group cohesion.

The wildebeest is a herd animal and relies on mutual protection from the other members of the group, especially when the females are giving birth. During the peak migration times, some 1.5 million wildebeest move across the African plains.

OPPOSITE   BAT ROOSTERS

Thousands of Southeastern brown bats roosting upside-down in a cave in Florida. Bats may spend half their lives in roosts. clustered together for warmth and protection from predators.

BELOW   CHOOSING A ROOST

A Geoffrey's bat at a communal roost in Germany. Roosting sites include crevices in rocks and trees, caves, mines, tree trunks, stems, and leaves, and the eaves and roofs of houses.

OPPOSITE PARTNERS FOR LIFE

The demoiselle crane is the smallest of the crane species and the second most abundant. It lives in dry grasslands in many parts of the world. Cranes form monogamous pair bonds and claim a territory in which to reproduce.

BELOW COASTAL BIRDS

The oystercatcher lives along the rocky shorelines and sandy beaches of the coasts of many parts of the world. It is a gregarious bird and flocks throughout the year, except during mating when pairs claim territories in which to breed.

ONE OR MANY

pp. 864–865

STORMS OF STARLINGS

Common starlings at dusk in England returning to roost. Thousands of birds often gather together in great swirling flocks.

COOT GATHERINGS

Coots are aquatic birds that live in wetlands. They can be gregarious, especially during the winter when thousands of them sometimes gather on lakes, or even on coastal waters. During this time many lazy coots feed by stealing food off their fellows, thus saving themselves the energy of deep-water diving for the plant material they gather from the bottoms of lakes and other wetlands.

ONE OR MANY

Pelicans are found on most of the world's seas
(on all continents except Antarctica) and on
many inland waters, too. The ones shown here
are in Florida (above) and Africa (below). They
are highly gregarious birds that live in vast
colonies. Some co-operate to fish, forming a
line to chase schools of small fish into the
shallows where they can scoop them up
with their giant beaks.

GREGARIOUS WADERS

Flamingos are gregarious wading birds that live in large flocks in aquatic areas where they feed on shellfish and algae. They produce a single chick which both parents nurse as it feeds on a special "milk" the flamingos produce.

pp. 872–873

SUPER-COLONIES

Young flamingos live in groups of up to 300,000 birds. Other large flocks mass in areas of brackish or salty waters or on alkaline lakes where their numbers can exceed a million birds.

TRAVELERS

About half the bird species in the world spend their summers and winters in different locations. Here, snow geese flock for their semi-annual trip.

pp. 876–877

GREAT ROOKERIES

A colony of gannets on a rock in Cape St. Mary, in New-foundland, Canada. This is one of the largest and most spectacular gannet rookeries in the world.

The Clark's nutcracker lives in coniferous forests, usually above 4000 feet (1200 m) where it feeds on pine seeds, insects, berries, fruits, and small mammals. It is a gregarious bird and often gathers in large flocks.

BELOW   A MEDITERRANEAN SONGBIRD

The Sardinian warbler lives all over the Mediterranean basin, feeding on insects and fruit. It is a songbird with a long and melodious song.

pp. 880–881 WADERS ON THE WING

A large flock of curlews on the wing. Curlews are wading birds with brown plumage and long downward curving beaks.

OPPOSITE EAGLE MIGRATION

The short-toed eagle lives in the Mediterranean basin, Russia, the Middle East, India, and Indonesia. These birds of prey migrate in small groups to avoid the winter chill.

BELOW EYES IN THE BACK OF ITS HEAD?

The northern hawk owl is so named because it behaves more like a hawk than an owl. These owls are generally monogamous.

pp. 884–885 SHOULDER TO SHOULDER

A colony of king penguins on South Georgia Island, Antarctica. These birds nest in groups of up to 10,000 individuals; the penguins huddle close but not too close, to avoid any flipper slaps or beak jabs from a cross neighbor!

MODERN-DAY DRAGON

The Komodo dragon is a solitary creature that lives on Komodo Island and nearby islands, in Indonesia. Growing up to 10 feet (3 m) in length, it is the world's largest lizard. It has up to 60 very sharp teeth which are swarming with virulent bacteria so that even if a victim survives an attack it will die later of infection.

ONE OR MANY

pp. 888–889   A MASS OF SNAKES

A mass of juvenile Gulf coast ribbon snakes in Texas. These nervous and fast moving snakes grow up to nearly three feet (1 m) long and are commonly found near water. Up to 80 young may develop inside a female snake's body and are born fully formed. In spring, in northern regions, huge numbers come out of hibernation and congregate en masse to mate.

OPPOSITE   SWEETLIPS

These lined sweetlips inhabit ribbon reefs on the Great Barrier Reef in Australia and other tropical coastlines. The goldstriped sweetlips has narrow yellow stripes on its head and body and often swims in groups during the day. They are found in the sea close to Japanese islands and near Australia and New Caledonia.

ABOVE   BANNERFISH

A shoal of longfin bannerfish near Rangiroa Atoll, French Polynesia, South Pacific Ocean. They live in sheltered coastal bays and coral reef waters — in reef channels, faces and slopes, and in deep lagoons where they swim in pairs or in small schools.

ONE OR MANY

pp. 892–893 CATFISH SHOAL

A shoal of striped catfish in the Indo-Pacific. These nocturnal fish move in dense schools, mainly in tropical bays and estuaries or in deep water in rivers and streams.

OPPOSITE BARRACUDA SCHOOL

Chevron barracuda fish schooling at Yap, Micronesia. These fish have long silver bodies with chevron-shaped bar markings and live in tropical Indo-Pacific seas. Young barracudas usually hunt in small groups close to shore.

BELOW AGGRESSIVE BULL SHARKS

A group of menacing bull sharks in the Bahamas. The bull shark will eat almost anything and is very aggressive. It is one of the most frequent attackers of people.

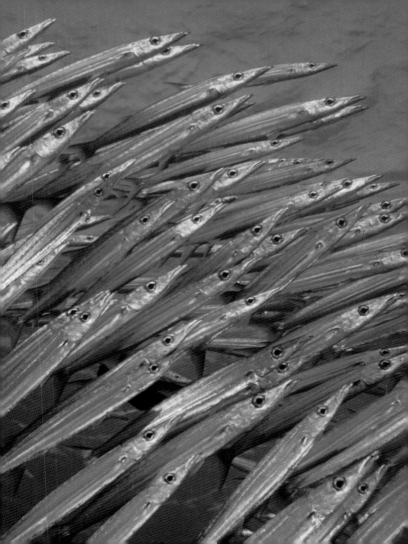

ONE OR MANY

pp. 896–897 HUMPBACKS BUBBLE-NET FEEDING

A group of humpback whales bubble-net feeding for herring off Frederick Sound, in Alaska. They work together to herd fish by blowing sheets of bubble curtains to confuse and trap the fish.

OPPOSITE   MONARCH MIGRATION

From August to October, millions of monarch butterflies migrate vast distances — some 2,500 miles (4,000 km) from Canada and the northeastern United States to California and Mexico, following the same routes every year.

ABOVE   FOLLOW THE LEADER

Pine procession caterpillars are so-named because they often form long, single-file lines of caterpillars and blindly follow their leader.

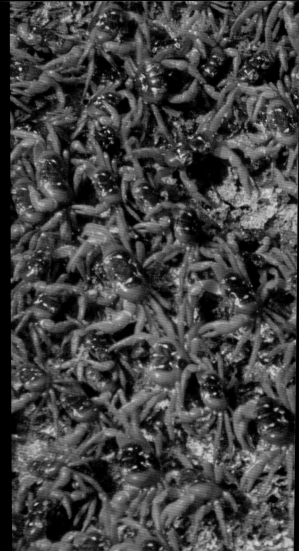

A CROWD OF CRABS

A vast crowd of Pacific Christmas Island red crabs spawning on the beach. About 120 million of these red crabs live in shady sites on the island. Most are bright red but there is the occasional orange one and, even more rarely, a purple crab.

pp. 902–903

OFF FOR A DIP

These Christmas Island red crab adults are off to take a dip in the sea to replenish their body salts and moisture before reproduction. They are sexually mature at five years old when they begin to participate in these mass breeding migrations.

ONE OR MANY

JELLYFISH GIANTS

This is a huge cloud of Mastigias jellyfish in the Western Pacific Islands. Some individuals may grow to be 3 feet (1 m) in length. They are nearly always to be found in a group close to the surface, where they feed on microplankton.

olor can serve many different purposes in the animal kingdom. Mostly it provides camouflage, helping the animal to blend in with its surroundings and making it less visible to predators. Sometimes there is even a color difference between males and females of the same species. Among birds, for example, the female is often a dull green or brown because she is the one who will spend days or weeks

COLOR

sitting on the nest to incubate eggs so she must be as inconspicuous as possible. The male, on the other hand, is often glamorously clad in bright feathers that serve to attract a partner during courtship. We have already seen that some animals exploit color to warn predators that they are poisonous or foul tasting; other innocuous animals imitate the colors of their more dangerous cousins to fool predators into thinking they too should be avoided.

pp. 906–907   YELLOW YOUTH

This bright yellow snake is a juvenile green tree python from Papua New Guinea and the northwestern tip of Australia. The young pythons are yellow or red but turn green at about six months.

OPPOSITE   SCARLET NOSES

West African male mandrills have brightly colored faces and rumps. Their noses are a bright red and their white cheeks can be vivid blue.

BELOW   FUR OF GOLD

The golden snub-nosed monkey of China has long golden fur that is greatly prized by many and is sometimes used to make coats.

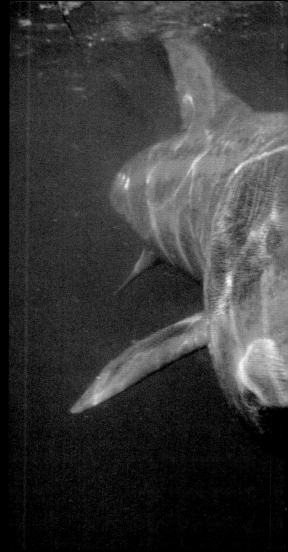

pp. 710–711 GRAZERS

A bullethead parrotfish grazes on coral in the Red Sea, Egypt. It uses its beak to rasp algae, polyps, and other small plant and animal life from the surface of coral and rock. It also eats seaweed and mollusks. The grinding teeth in its throat help to break up food ready for digestion.

BIGMOUTH SHARK

The basking shark, also known as a bigmouth shark, glides along with its mouth wide open. It is a filter feeder and its gill rakers filter out everything that enters it mouth except plankton, fish eggs, and baby fish. Digestion is rapid and the food soon becomes a soupy reddish mass

pp. 714–715 SURGEONFISH

A green turtle being cleaned by surgeonfish (named for the razor sharp spines at the base of their bodies that can cut like a knife).

OPPOSITE A FULL TIME JOB

A giant tortoise feeding on Santa Cruz Island in the Galapagos. These giants spend most of their waking hours grazing and browsing.

BELOW A VARIED DIET

This hood (or saddleback) tortoise lives on Hood Island in the Galapagos. The Galapagos giant tortoise eats a wide variety of vegetation, including grass and vines, cactus fruit, and both the fallen fruits and spiny pads of the prickly pear.

FINDING FOOD

OPEN WIDE

A brown water snake stretches its jaws wide to swallow a catfish in the Everglades National Park, in Florida. Water snakes hunt by day at the water's edge for fish, frogs, worms, leeches, crayfish, young turtles, salamanders, and small birds and mammals. At night, they catch small fish in shallow water, such as minnows.

pp. 720–721

PREDATORY LIZARD

A darkling beetle serves as a tasty meal for a collared lizard in Colorado. This predatory lizard often hunts in an upright position, running on its hind legs. It preys on grasshoppers, beetles, spiders, and small snakes and lizards.

Whenever an animal is born, the game of life begins anew. Every young creature must learn to escape predators, find food, and reproduce. Animals have many different ways of avoiding attack, including speed, camouflage, threatening postures, well-developed sight, smell, and hearing, the defensive use of poison, armor, horns, teeth, and spines, posting guards, playing

SURVIVAL

dead, or simply hiding away. The environment itself can also be hostile and special skills or attributes are required, for example, to survive extremes of cold and heat, lack or short supply of food and water, or the arrival of new predators or competitors for resources in a given habitat. Sadly, the greatest threat of all to animals is posed by mankind's inability or unwillingness to share our planet's resources.

A rhinoceros horn is made of keratin, the same material as fingernails and hair. It is a useful defensive weapon for the animal but some people believe it has aphrodisiac and medicinal powers. This has led to over-hunting, threatening the survival of the rhinoceros.

OPPOSITE NO PLACE TO CALL HOME

The aye aye is another endangered species. As the forests of Madagascar are cleared for growing sugar cane and coconut, the aye-aye loses its habitat.

BELOW A SHRINKING HABITAT

Tarsiers are tiny, nocturnal, forest-dwelling primates; at one time found in Asia, Europe, and North America, they now survive on just a few islands in Southeast Asia.

ABOVE THE MEANEST AND THE BEST

Male chacma baboons, like this one in Botswana, engage in aggressive threat displays to establish who ranks highest in their group's social hierarchy.

OPPOSITE OPEN WIDE

A crested macaque gives a fine yawn display in the Sulawesi, Indonesia. The males' huge yawns reveal an impressive array of canines in order to assert dominance and avoid conflict.

Attitudes to life vary with the season. In the winter, finding enough food and simply surviving takes precedence for red deer in northern Europe. In the warmer months, however, rutting, mating, and raising young predominate.

A Kirk's colobus monkey feeding in a reserve in Zanzibar. Rapid population growth has restricted these monkeys to a small part of the island. Many are hit by cars as the lack of trees forces them down to the ground where they are also more vulnerable to natural enemies such as chimpanzees.

A Japanese macaque in Japan. Macaques are the most widespread primate, ranging from northern Africa to Japan. These creatures are highly adaptable and this serves them well in the survival stakes.

TREE HOMES

Tree kangaroos are adapted for life in the trees. These strange creatures live in Australia and New Guinea. They appear to have evolved from animals similar to modern kangaroos since they retain features, such as powerful hind legs, that make them suitable for life on the ground. But they have also evolved features to suit their new arboreal homes, such as long tails which they use for balance.

AVOIDING DANGER

Armadillos, like the three-banded armadillo shown here, have excellent defenses to ensure their survival in their Central and South American homes. They often hide in burrows when they sense a danger, but if they meet an enemy head on, will curl up in their bony "coats of armor" until the predator is gone.

**NO SNEAKING UP
ON THIS BABY**

This Demidoff's
bushbaby lives in the
rainforests of the
Democratic Republic
of Congo. This
nocturnal animal has
large eyes and ears
that help it to both
see and hear in the
dark. Although its
eyes are fixed in their
sockets, a bushbaby
can rotate its head
nearly 180 degrees in
order to see what is
going on all around.

A hedgehog crossing the road and a porcupine displaying its quills. Both hedgehogs and porcupines rely on a barrier of fearsome spines to discourage attack by predators. When threatened, they curl up into a ball inside this protective shield. Unfortunately, in areas now criss-crossed with roads, this is not a good way for them to defend themselves against an oncoming car or truck and many are killed on the roads.

SURVIVING THE WINTER

Deer in deep winter snow.
Deer in the far north grow a
thick, warm winter coat every
year to insulate themselves
against the cold. Low
temperatures, freezing winds,
and ice make extra demands on
their metabolisms so they build
up body fat, both as extra
protection and as a source of
energy. They move around less
to conserve this energy and
generally stay among evergreen
trees where it is a few degrees
warmer than out in the open.

A deer's antlers may look like formidable weapons but they are generally used for fighting within the herd during the rut and as proof of masculinity rather than for defense against outsiders. Deer survive mainly by being elusive and shy, keeping a low profile and being fleet of hoof when needs be.

BELOW KEEPING COOL

The summer heat brings another set of problems. This deer is sitting in a pond in an attempt both to cool off and discourage irritating flies.

WINTER WOOLIES

An Abruzzi chamois kid in its shaggy winter coat in the Abruzzi national Park, in central Italy. These unique animals, which once ranged over much of the Italian Apennines, are now critically endangered and less than 1000 individuals are believed to be living in the wild.

pp. 744–745

SHAGGY WINTER COATS

American bison have
thick shaggy coats to
help them survive
the icy winters.
They can also move
quickly and may
stampede when
threatened. Free-
roaming herds
migrate hundreds of
miles and, when they
need to, can run at
about 40 miles
(65 km) per hour.

DANGER IN THE BUSH

The Cape buffalo is
regarded as one of
the most dangerous
and unpredictable
animals in Africa.
Often a herd of these
buffalo will work
together to "mob"
a predator such
as a lion.

Contrary to popular belief, porcupines are not able to throw their quills.
But they do swish their quilled tails at attackers and if the victim comes into
contact with a quill then it may be driven into the predator's skin. The quills
are barbed and therefore difficult and painful to extract. This crested
porcupine is scavenging on the ground in central Kenya. Its back quills
can be raised into a crest.

OPPOSITE   MARCH HARES

Hares are almost invisible during courtship in the long spring grass.
Like rabbits, hares breed prolifically with some species producing
2 to 4 litters throughout the year.

ABOVE   CAMOUFLAGE

Hares can blend in perfectly with their surroundings making them difficult
for predators to see.

A family of strikingly colored douc langur monkeys, from the forests of Cambodia, Vietnam, and Laos. These highly endangered monkeys are captured for sale as pets.

OPPOSITE STOP THIEF!

A patas monkey kidnaps a baby patas and makes a run for it. With their dark eye-patches, these monkeys certainly look the part of the villain.

BELOW BLACK AND WHITE BEAUTY

An eastern black and white colobus mother with her pure white baby. These African monkeys have been hunted for their beautiful pelts which are sold as wall decorations.

WHY DO ZEBRAS HAVE STRIPES?

Zebras engaged in mutual grooming. The zebra's splendid markings may at first seem to make them stand out. But in the hazy dust and heat of the African savanna and scrublands, they may actually help to make them less visible. Some scientists also think that when a herd of zebra moves together the stripes will confuse predators, making it difficult to for them to distinguish one animal from the next.

Little is known of the okapi, a horse-like member of the giraffe family that lives deep in the rainforests of central Africa. It has striped legs that some scientists believe provide a "follow me" imprinting signal to calves so that they don't get lost in the thick jungle.

BELOW   A HANDSOME BUCK

A male blackbuck resting in India. The males have long spiral horns and darker coloring than the females, but they both blend in beautifully with the semi-desert to open woodland habitats that they occupy.

COLOR

MALES AND FEMALES

The nyala is a spiral-horned antelope that lives in riverside thicket and dense vegetation in southeast Africa. Males (right) and females (below) differ in size and coloring. The male is much larger, with long horns, and a dark coat with white stripes. The smaller female is reddish brown with white stripes.

Unfortunately for the leopard, its beautiful coat with its gold background overlaid with black and red markings has always been a major fashion statement. Hunting and loss of habitat to farming have put all leopard species on the endangered animals list.

OPPOSITE   SMALL CAT FUR TRADE

The solitary ocelot is a small cat that lives in the forests of Central and South America. Its fur resembles that of the jaguar and it has been hunted extensively for this reason.

BELOW   CATS IN THE SAND

Sand cats live in arid regions of North Africa, the Middle East, and Central Asia. Their pale gold fur blends in with the rocks and sands of their native environment.

CROWING ABOUT IT

A pair of capercaille in a taiga forest in Finland. The male, or cock, capercaille is much larger than the female and has shiny dark plumage with some white markings. The hen is smaller with a beautiful mottled plumage of grey, orange, yellow, black, and green that helps her blend into the woods. Here the male is displaying during courtship by fanning out his tail feathers, raising his wings, pointing his beak skyward, and calling.

INDIGO PARROTS

A pair of hyacinth macaws show their striking blue-indigo plumage. These large parrots live in Brazil, Bolivia, and Paraguay. They are an endangered species in the wild.

A male red-winged parrot eating seeds in the bush in Australia. These parrots often feed by hanging upside down; this may make them less easy for predators to distinguish.

COLOR

OPPOSITE GANG GANG COCKATOO

A male gang gang cockatoo in Australia. These parrots range throughout southeastern Australia and Tasmania. The male gang gang has a red head and crest while the female has a smaller grey crest.

BELOW A MAJOR MITCHELL

A male pink cockatoo with its trademark elegant pick crest. These Australian parrots are also known as Major Mitchells after a 19th-century explorer who raved about their beauty.

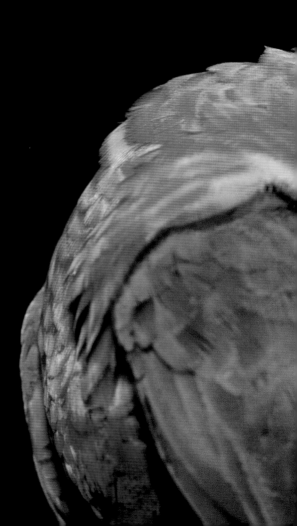

LOVEBIRDS

A pair of lovebirds perched and ready to preen. Most lovebirds are a bright emerald green with rosy faces but some are different colors. Like most parrots, lovebirds form monogamous pairs.

A NOISY RAINBOW

A rainbow lorikeet preening its brightly colored plumage. Even its underwings are brightly colored and it displays these to full effect when in flight, all the while screeching raucously.

ABOVE   A KEEN FISHERBIRD

A kingfisher watches the world go by in India. These birds have dazzling plumage in vibrant green, turquoise, cinnamon, and cobalt blue. They fly rapidly, skimming over still or slow-moving waters as they hunt fish.

OPPOSITE   LILY TROTTERS

This American purple gallinule lives in the everglades of Florida but these birds are also found in other parts of the United States, Central and South America, and the West Indies. A brightly colored bird about the size of a chicken, it tiptoes across lily pads on the marshes.

pp. 936–937 A TOUCH OF ACID YELLOW

A king penguin pair stand face to face on Possession Island in the sub-Antarctic. The conventional image of penguins is of a sharp symphony in black and white but these birds have the added vibrancy of acid yellow on the throat, neck, and beak.

OPPOSITE COURTING COLORS

This large spectacular saddlebill stork lives in Kruger National Park, South Africa. Both sexes of these brightly colored birds have a yellow saddle-shaped patch on the upper part of the beak. Their courtship involves the pair running about with their wings spread to expose their fine plumage.

ABOVE BIG PINK BILL

An Australian pelican in Queensland. This is Australia's largest flying bird. It has a long pink bill, black and white feathers, and a bright yellow ring encircling each eye. It uses its rather saggy throat pouch as a collecting point for fish and tadpoles.

OPPOSITE   A COLOR FOR EVERY MOOD

The red-eyed tree frog has huge scarlet eyes and a very bright green body with sky-blue and creamy-yellow stripes on its sides. These frogs can change their color to darker green or reddish brown, according to their mood.

BELOW   BEAUTIFUL BUT DEADLY

The blue poison arrow frog lives in the rainforests of Suriname. Their color can range from powder blue to cobalt and sapphire blue. They also have black spots. They secrete their deadly poison through their skins.

The coral snake — in this case an Arizona coral snake — is deadly poisonous. Predators recognize the coral snake by the characteristic pattern of its red, yellow, and black markings. They know just how lethal this snake is and give it a wide berth.

BELOW   A LESS NOXIOUS IMITATOR

The false coral snake is only mildly poisonous but its markings are very similar to its deadlier cousin. Predators leave these snakes alone too because they think that it may be a real coral snake.

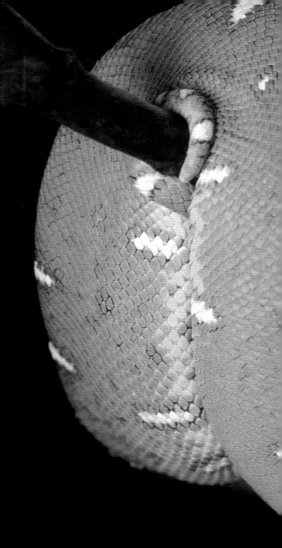

AN EMERALD BOA

The emerald tree boa lives in the rainforests of the Amazon basin and in Venezuela, Guyana, and Suriname. Its skin is bright green with white markings. This coloration mimics the leaves marked with mold or bird droppings among which it lives, providing a good disguise for sneaking up on the birds and mammals on which it feeds. This snake's jaws are attached to each other by stretchy ligaments, allowing it to swallow surprisingly large prey. These snakes don't chew their victims, they just swallow them whole. Strong acids in their stomachs break them down into food.

COLOR

The eyelash viper, like this one in Ecuador, is named for the enlarged scale it has above each eye, giving the appearance of an eyelash. It can be yellow, or reddish-yellow, grey-brown, or green. The yellow vipers may be spotted with white, black, or red; the darker ones can have black or red spots.

BELOW   AN ORANGE EMERALD BOA

A young emerald tree boa coiled around a branch in Guyana. Its parents are bright green but the live-born (these snakes do not hatch from eggs) juveniles are deep orange-brown with white spots.

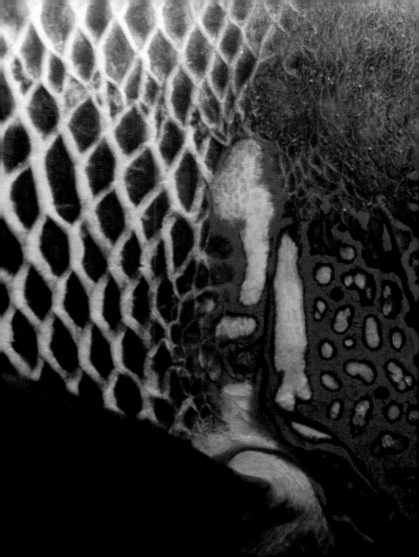

pp. 948–949 THE FACE OF AN ANGEL

Blue face angelfish live in the warm eastern waters of the Pacific. This one is on the Great Barrier Reef, near Australia. These yellow and blue fish have a reticulated pattern in which blue predominates. They also have a yellow mask over the eyes and a false eye on the dorsal fin. The juveniles are black with vertical blue and white lines.

OPPOSITE LOLLING IN THE CORAL

Orange fin anemonefish resting in soft coral. The body is usually brown to black with two white-to-blue bars. The dorsal fin is an orange or yellow hue and the tail is white. This fish lives in the tropical marine waters of the western Pacific, generally seeking sanctuary among the tentacles of an anemone. It feeds mainly on plankton and algae.

ABOVE WHAT A SWEETY

A yellow ribbon sweetlips in the waters of Indonesia. These fish inhabit protected lagoons and seaward reefs in the Pacific Ocean, from the west coast of India and the Philippines to New Guinea and northern Australia. The fine blue and yellow stripes really do look like ribbons.

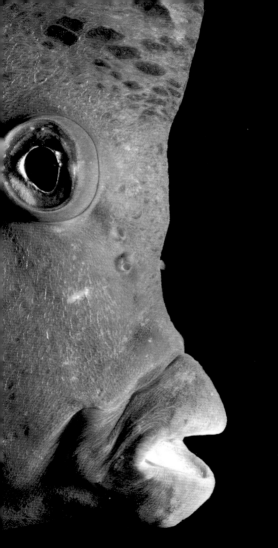

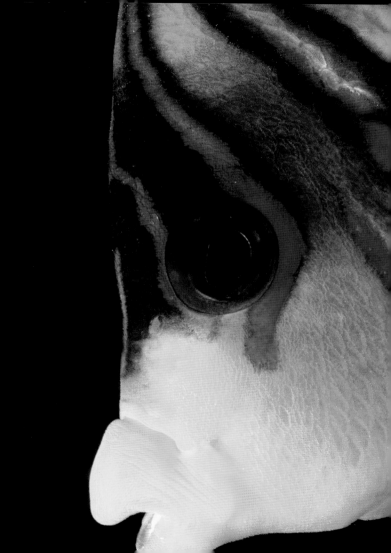

This longnose
hawkfish is in sea
fan coral near the
Sulawesi, Indonesia.
It has a white body
with red horizontal
and vertical striping
to give a checkered
effect. In among the
red gorgonian sea
fan coral it is almost
invisible.

FINAL GLORY

Sockeye salmon
swimming upriver to
spawn in Canada.
Breeding males
develop a humped
back and both sexes
turn a brilliant dark
red on the back and
sides, with pale olive-
green heads and
upper jaws. This is
their final glory for
they will die a few
weeks after
spawning.

The weedy sea dragon, also known as the common sea dragon, lives in the coastal waters of southern Australia. The sea dragon is a close relative of the seahorse. It varies in color from reddy-brown to yellowish-green with iridescent blue bands on the upper body. Its pretty, seaweed-like fins and coloring help it to blend in with the seaweed and kelp among which it lives. Although not as rare as the leafy sea dragon, this species is also protected.

Nudibranchs are sea slugs. They have no shell to protect themselves but many are able to absorb the poisons of sea anemones or other creatures and use it against predators who try to eat them. Their very bright colors are meant as a warning to predators reminding them that they are poisonous. These nudibranchs (right) are mating near Sulawesi, Indonesia. Although hermaphroditic they cannot fertilize themselves so have to find a partner.

BELOW SALLY LIGHTFOOTS

Sally lightfoot crabs live in the Galapagos Islands and gained this name because of the way they move very quickly out of harm's way. These fiery red crabs are clearly visible just at the water's edge. Younger ones are born black to blend in with the lava but will turn an ever brighter red as they grow larger and reach maturity.

shores. They can be blue-green, turquoise, black, tan, yellow, or orange, and are a darker shade by day than by night. During courtship, the males wave their oversized claws high in the air and tap on the ground to impress the females.

CATERPILLARS THAT
LOOK LIKE FLOWERS

Caterpillars, like
these slug moth
caterpillars, make a
tasty meal for birds
and many other
predators. Slow
moving and with
no shell to protect
themselves, they rely
on being hard to see.

pp. 968–969
EMERGING BEAUTY

Two butterflies
emerging from their
chrysalides to reveal
their beautiful wings.
On the left, a poplar
admiral butterfly and
on the right a
morpho butterfly.

I N D E X

Page numbers in **BOLD** refer to pictures.

PICTURE CREDITS

The Publisher would like to thank the following for their kind permission to reproduce their photographs.

Aflo/naturepl.com: **675**; Doug Allan/naturepl.com: **242–3, 320–1**; Karl Ammann/naturepl.com: **339, 454, 456–7, 680, 774–5**; Terry Andrewartha/naturepl.com: **674, 704**; Ingo Arndt/naturepl.com: **29, 34–5, 37, 116–7, 189, 205, 251, 330–1, 384, 450–1, 538–9, 729, 920–1, 966–7**; Eric Baccega/naturepl.com: **358, 360–1, 374, 492–3, 936–7**; Claudio Bagnoli/Panda Photo: **942**; Paul Beinssen Lonely Planet Images: **168–9**; Niall Benvie/naturepl.com: **25, 135, 198, 206, 736, 750**; Peter Blackwell/naturepl.com: **376–7, 681, 748–9**; Tom Brakefield The Image Works: **144–5**; Hermann Brehm/naturepl.com: **642**; Mark Brownlow/naturepl.com: **732–3**; Jane Burton/naturepl.com: **502**; Pete Cairns/naturepl.com: **430**; John Cancalosi/naturepl.com: **255, 427, 439, 586–7, 632, 702–3, 720–1, 802, 943**; Giuliano Cappelli, Florence: **8–9, 14–21, 38–42, 48–9, 54–69, 72–77, 80–1, 88–105, 112–3 120, 122–3, 128–9, 132–3, 136–8, 140–1, 147, 150–5, 161–2, 164–7, 170–1, 176–7, 208–10, 216–9, 230–7, 239, 254, 260–1, 268–70, 274–5, 278–81, 296–302, 304–5, 308–15, 322–3, 342–43, 346, 348–9, 350–5, 359, 362, 364–5, 370–3, 378–9, 394–9, 418–21, 424–5, 428–9, 460–5, 467–77, 484–91, 494–5, 503–21, 524, 553, 556–7, 560–1, 564–9, 574–5, 580–1, 584–5, 590–5, 602–3, 607–11, 624–6, 628–31, 633–5, 646–7, 654–73, 676–7, 686–701, 705, 737–47, 751, 758–9, 762–69, 776, 778–9, 782–7, 796–9, 832, 834–43, 845–7, 849–59, 863, 866–82**; Mark Carwardine/naturepl.com: **382–3, 907**; Bernard Castelein/naturepl.com: **174, 916, 934**; Brandon Cole: **4–5, 10, 82–3, 86, 106–7, 196–7, 292–3, 500–1, 638–9, 818–9, 825, 894, 896–7, 950, 962**; Andrew Cooper/naturepl.com: **606**; Christophe Courteau/naturepl.com: **240–1, 258**; Bill Curtsinger/Overseas: **160**; Bruce Davidson/naturepl.com: **228–9, 333, 385, 598, 619, 734–5, 752–3, 917**; Gertrud & Helmut Denzau/naturepl.com: **922**; Georgette Douwma/naturepl.com: **335, 498–9, 529, 706–11, 804, 956–7, 965**; John Downer/naturepl.com: **264, 271, 327, 789**; Richard Du Toit/naturepl.com: **44–5, 130–1, 148–9, 211, 366, 408–9, 552, 754**; Michael Durham/naturepl.com: **6–7, 201, 926**; Klaus Echle/naturepl.com: **615**; Hanne & Jens Eriksen/naturepl.com: **640–1, 884–5**; Justine Evans/naturepl.com: **204**; Jeff Foott/naturepl.com: **11, 222–3, 225, 226–7, 570–1, 614, 616–7, 622–3, 678, 682–3, 718–9, 958–9**; Jurgen Freund/naturepl.com: **252–3, 326, 824, 892–3, 900–1, 902–3**; Martin Gabriel/naturepl.com: **724**; Nick Garbutt/naturepl.com: **844**; Laurent Geslin/naturepl.com: **541**; Jose Luis Gomez De Francisco/naturepl.com: **214–5**; Nick Gordon/naturepl.com: **600–1**; David Hall/naturepl.com: **386–7, 532, 810–1, 960, 961**; Graham Hatherley/naturepl.com: **760–1**; Tony Heald/naturepl.com: **220, 221, 402–3, 627, 918–9, 939**; Rachel Hingley/naturepl.com: **525**; Ashok Jain/naturepl.com: **238, 406–7, 884**; Alan James/naturepl.com: **712–3**; Hans Christoph Kappel/naturepl.com: **286, 968**; David Kjaer/naturepl.com: **303, 424, 558–9, 862, 864–5**; Brian Lightfoot/naturepl.com: **183–4**; Fabio Liverani/naturepl.com: **816–7**; Neil Lucas/naturepl.com: **178–9, 184–5, 212–3**; Jorma Luhta/naturepl.com: **924–5**; Bengt Lundberg/naturepl.com: **50–1, 597**; George McCarthy/naturepl.com: **612–3, 790–1**; Mary McDonald/naturepl.com: **114–5, 256–7, 282, 411**; Barry Mansell/naturepl.com: **536–7, 589, 861**; Tim Martin/naturepl.com: **367**; Steven David Miller/naturepl.com: **26, 644–5, 800–1, 928, 932–3, 948–9**; Marco Nardi, Florence: **22–23, 32–33, 125, 156–7**; Owen Newman/naturepl.com: **347**; Dietmar Nill/naturepl.com: **142, 244–5, 290–1, 306–7, 325, 368–9, 434–5, 466, 684, 685, 780–1, 822–3, 860**; Xi Zhi Nong/naturepl.com: **908**; Rolf Nussbaumer/naturepl.com: **416–7, 888–9**; Ben Osborne/naturepl.com: **522–3**; Pete Oxford/naturepl.com: **2–3, 119, 143, 175, 182, 192–3, 288, 294–5, 328–9, 336–7, 344–5, 363, 375, 393, 440–1, 445, 458, 496, 527, 599, 650–1, 679, 716, 728, 777, 792–3, 803, 812, 828–9, 909, 923, 944–5, 946–7, 969**; Andrew Parkinson/naturepl.com: **316–7, 726, 772–3**; Mark Payne–Gill/naturepl.com: **940**; Doug Perrine/naturepl.com: **108–9, 263, 528, 530–1, 533, 714–5, 890–1, 952–3**; Constantinos Petrinos/naturepl.com: **437, 808–9, 818, 963**; Tony Phelps/naturepl.com: **442–3, 805**; David Pike/naturepl.com: **13, 481**; Michael Pitts/naturepl.com: **248–9, 289, 636–7, 886–7, 895, 904–5, 951**; Mike Potts/naturepl.com: **380–1**; Roger Powell/naturepl.com: **883, 929**; Peter Reese/naturepl.com: **432–3**; T.J. Rich/naturepl.com: **287, 324**; Gabriel Rojo/naturepl.com: **412–3**; Jeff Rotman/naturepl.com: **1, 158–9, 194–5, 250, 259, 388–9, 806–7, 814–5, 820–1, 954–5**; Jose B. Ruiz/naturepl.com: **356–7, 390–1**; Francois Savigny/naturepl.com: **576–7**; Phil Savoie/naturepl.com: **111, 190–1, 426, 534–5, 941**; Carine Schrurs/naturepl.com: **436**; Peter Scoones/naturepl.com: **199**; Anup Shah/naturepl.com: **36, 43, 52–3, 70–1, 78–9, 126–7, 202–3, 266–7, 338, 400–1, 410, 446, 452–3, 455, 461, 480–1, 482–3, 478–9, 542–3, 546, 547, 544–5, 550–1, 548–9, 554–5, 562–3, 582–3, 648–9, 652–3, 723, 756–7, 830–1, 910–5**; David Shale/naturepl.com: **438, 813**; Geoff Simpson/naturepl.com: **186–7**; Toby Sinclair/naturepl.com: Cover; Marguerite Smits Van Oyen/naturepl.com: **618, 755**; Lynn M. Stone/naturepl.com: **146, 163, 318–9, 572–3, 617, 725, 770–1, 833, 848**; Kim Taylor/naturepl.com: **643, 930–1**; David Tipling/naturepl.com: **496–7, 526**; Robert Valentic/naturepl.com: **794–5**; Claudio Velasquez/naturepl.com: **188**; Tom Vezo/naturepl.com: **447, 717, 935, 964**; Carol Walker/naturepl.com: **272–3**; Tom Walmsley/naturepl.com: **87**; John Waters/naturepl.com: **620–1**; Dave Watts/naturepl.com: **265, 276–7, 340–1, 404–5, 414–5, 604–5, 918, 927**; Doug Wechsler/naturepl.com: **110, 588, 788**; David Welling/naturepl.com: **173**; Doc White/naturepl.com: **46–7, 84–5**; Staffan Widstrand/naturepl.com: **134, 172, 207, 283, 827, 938**; Mike Wilkes/naturepl.com: **422–3, 536**; Rod Williams/naturepl.com: **30–1, 121, 180–1**; Solvin Zankl/naturepl.com: **246–7, 727**.